Michael's Roses

Michael's Roses

✦

A Chronicle of an American Family that has Made History from Early Colonial America of 1654 to the Present Day

Roland A. Dwinell

iUniverse, Inc.

New York Lincoln Shanghai

Michael's Roses
A Chronicle of an American Family that has Made History from Early Colonial America of 1654 to the Present Day

iUniverse books may be ordered through booksellers or by contacting:

iUniverse
2021 Pine Lake Road, Suite 100
Lincoln, NE 68512
www.iuniverse.com
1-800-Authors (1-800-288-4677)

Because of the dynamic nature of the Internet, any Web addresses or links contained in this book may have changed since publication and may no longer be valid.

The views expressed in this work are solely those of the author and do not necessarily reflect the views of the publisher, and the publisher hereby disclaims any responsibility for them.

ISBN: 978-0-595-45091-6 (pbk)
ISBN: 978-0-595-89402-4 (ebk)

Printed in the United States of America

This book is dedicated to my wife, Dr. Ann J. Dwinell. She is the heart of our family. Like so many Dwinell women before her, she has sustained the bond that has made our line of descent of the Dwinell family continue. The family is in good hands, now, because she is here. It will be in good hands in the future, because the memory of her contribution will continue.

"If you have built castles in the air, your work need not be lost; that is where they should be. Now put foundations under them."

—Henry David Thoreau

Contents

Prologue

There are many ways to approach history. Typically, history is played on a stage of political and military events. Kings, queens, emperors, presidents and other renowned political leaders are mentioned with generals and diplomats in geo-political and power-political terms. Explorers find distant lands to enhance these geo-political aims of the state.

Whether they are heroes or despots, these people who play these varied roles adorn history books. Kings, queens, emperors and presidents rule people. The people who are ruled do what the political leader dictates. Generals, explorers and ship commanders carry out the dictates of political leaders. As a result, well known men emerge as heroes. The sweep of history suggests that events occur, for good or evil, at the behest of these noted participants.

The theme of this book is that historical events occur because of the actions of ordinary people. These actions, sometimes free sometimes otherwise, occur because ordinary people follow the leadership of these rulers. Without this following, the leadership structure of a given nation would advance its cause, however noble or ignoble, at its peril.

The scope of this book spans history from feudal Europe to the democratic, capitalist environment of the United State of America. One branch of a family that had its American beginning in Colonial America is traced from its origins in Europe to the present day. The journey of this family through the centuries relates a story of the development of one region of a nation as its civilization was literally carved out of a wilderness.

There was a pronounced and ever present class structure in feudal Europe of the seventeenth century. The citizens of the various European nations and political states were destined to remain in the social class to which they were born. Although this reality was advantageous to the titled class, the lower classes of each society had a bleaker outlook for their family and their descendants who would follow. The ruling or titled class dictated the political direction, economic decisions, military involvement, religion, mores and, essentially the daily lives of the lower or peasant class.

A new continent and, perhaps, a new life beckoned. We know of the various colonies that were established for religious and/or economic reasons. People came

1

for reasons of religious zeal and economic profit. Some people came as indentured servants with no organized belief or with a religious direction different than the mandated religion of the political state that hosted them. These people were destined, at least temporarily, to a life of servitude. Their short-term outlook was bleak.

If they could maintain a positive outlook for the duration of their servitude, they had the opportunity to lead a de facto life of freedom. These former servants could then join the ranks of the conventional colonists. In fact, they did.

So, the various elements of the American colonies came, and a civilization emerged. We will explore the life of colonists in the northeast corner of the Massachusetts Bay Colony as well as the lives of a specific family who continued to live through the generations in a New England Yankee environment. This family is the Dwinell family who had their American beginnings in Topsfield of the Massachusetts Bay Colony.

This family whose lives we will trace experienced many of the conditions prevalent in that span of history from 1654 to today. This story is about people who found themselves at various points in history in a New England environment. They responded. How they responded will help to explain how they survived. It will also help to explain how our civilization and independent nation grew to the society we enjoy today.

1

Michael—the Pioneer

○ ○
"After they have thus found out a place of abode, they burrow themselves into the earth for their first shelter, under some hill-side."[1]

—Captain Edward Johnson, London, 1654

We are indebted to a man named Henry Gale Dunnell, M.D., who in 1862 wrote "The True Genealogy of the Dunnel and Dwinell Family of New England."[2] This book is quite informative. Dr. Dunnell indicates that there are many variations to the name of the man we call Michael Dwinell, Senior. Michael Dwinell, Sr., is the pioneer of this story. This tendency to lack a clearly defined name was not surprising in the 1600s, but researchers indicate that Michael had an unusual number of name variations. Some variations of the name Dwinell include Donel, Doniel, Daniel, Duinell, Dwinel, Dunnell, Donnell and other variations that will be mentioned in the pages that follow.

Dr. Dunnell suggests that we should not be too certain of the origin of our name. He presents evidence that Michael did not provide us with a written version of his name. Essex County records of his will show that Michael left his mark as his signature. Interestingly, his mark bears a marked resemblance to a sketch of an apple.

Michael acquired land in Topsfield of the Massachusetts Bay Colony in 1672 conveyed via two deeds. There is no record of his signature on these deeds. The information came from the so-called Ipswich Deeds. The endnote will explain the circumstances. [3]

The name of the grantee on the deed is Mikal Donnell one of the name variations encountered in the research of this family. The grantee on this deed will

3

become significant as we pursue the Irish contention of Michael Dwinell, Sr.'s European origin.

There is an interesting version of this mark of Michael Dwinell as the signature on his will. A researcher named Frank Dwinell has a version of Michael's mark. His claim is that this mark may represent the Coat of Arms of the Count Do en el. In his Preface to his "1974 Reprint and Revision of the Genealogy of Ira Dwinell"[4] Frank has made some interesting but inconclusive observations about the origin of the Dwinell family.

Frank admits the inconclusive nature of his theory of our origin when he states Henry Dunnell "... could have easily been the father of Michael (Dwinell)" Henry Dunnell sailed on the merchant ship Bonaventure from England to the Virginia Colony in 1635.[5] Most accounts of Michael Dwinell indicate that he was born in either 1639 or 1640, so if Henry Dunnell were his father, Michael would have been born in America. The source that I used for this information indicates that many of these passengers to Virginia could have gone on to New England.

Frank Dwinell contends that our origin is Norman and the descendents of Count Do en el received considerable land holdings in Scotland, Ireland and England. Frank Dwinell suggests a connection to the House of Lancaster that needs to be explored. These observations add to the mystery of how Michael came to Topsfield. If his father were Henry Dunnell, Michael would have had to come from the Virginia Colony, given vital records suggesting his age and the evidence of Henry's voyage from England on the Bonaventure. Other theories will emerge as we discuss Michael Dwinell, Senior. You will become aware of a mystery that continues regarding his national origin.

Before we begin with Michael Dwinell, Senior, I should note that the current name of Dwinell has been Anglicized. My research has uncovered 35 variations (and counting) of the name on official records. No doubt each of us has many more variations of what we are called. Until my handwriting improved to its almost legible state, I would receive mail directed to a person named Divinell. Less than legible handwriting in an age and society without printed records could account for some of these variations. I had some difficulty reading handwritten Revolutionary War records in a Boxford, Massachusetts, Library source. Whatever his name or our difficulty in defining his origin, Michael Dwinell, Senior, did live in Topsfield of the Massachusetts Bay Colony. Let us go back in history to a sparsely settled portion of the Massachusetts Bay Colony where the story of Michael Dwinell in America began.

Let your imagination wander as we consider the only male alien Dwinell family member in our story. We can begin with the emergence of the man identified by most researchers until recently as a Frenchman, Michael Dwinell, Senior, my great, great, great, great, great, great grandfather. A little known legend in Topsfield has lasted, now, for more than 330 years. It is told that there was a rose bush 600 feet in from the road on Wenham Road in Topsfield. This rose bush is said to have bloomed each year since being planted by Michael when he first came to Topsfield.[6]

There are members of the Dwinell family who still live on Salem Road near Wenham Road in Topsfield. One of these members of the Dwinell family, Ruth Rebecca Dwinell Ingalls, has verified the existence of the rose bush of legend. She has told me that the rose bush lasted until the 1940s when it succumbed to the inevitable development of the area. Recently, I asked her where this bush was. She pointed to an area west of her home near the junction of Salem and Wenham Roads in Topsfield.

Part of Wenham Road appears to be Old Salem Road. As late as the early part of the 1900s there were substantial Dwinell land holdings in this area. There are at least two family descendents of Michael living on Salem Road today. Michael was the original owner of much of the Salem Road land in Topsfield. It should be noted that the Dwinell families in Topsfield together with the Appleton family of Ipswich may be the oldest families in New England to reside in the original land acquired by their ancestors more than eight generations ago.[7]

Scott Dwinell owns a Christmas tree farm on Salem Road. He brought me about 100 yards into his wood lot to show me the cellar of Michael's original home. The cellar remains are north of Salem Road.

The first reference I have found to our present name is that Michael received this Anglicized version of our name from the Reverend Joseph Capen,[8] an important minister in Topsfield and in the Salem area of the Massachusetts Bay Colony. When Michael's son, Michael, was born, the elder Michael became Michael Dwinell, Senior. It was a common practice for the English to Anglicize surnames.

The Dwinell clan has experienced the harshness of the Colonial experience, the French and Indian Wars, the rule of the English, the Revolutionary War that helped create our country and all that follows as the typical New England experience of our country unfolded. The Dwinell family has played a significant part in this historical journey as Michael's roses have continued to bloom. These experiences began on Old Salem Road in Topsfield of the Massachusetts Bay Colony.

References to the specific location of Old Salem Road have it going past the Dwinell house. The Dwinell house was owned by Michael Dwinell, Senior, who is described as a French immigrant in the Town Records of Topsfield. These same town records relate that Michael became a commoner on March 7, 1675/6.[9]

As a point of reference, you will note that two years are often mentioned to denote the time of an event. In 1582 Pope Gregory XIII instituted the Gregorian calendar to reflect the solar year. This convention replaced the Julian calendar named after the Roman emperor. The Julian calendar had been used since early Roman times. The difference in the two calendars was about ten days. Thus, two years are often used to denote the year of an occurrence soon after the Gregorian calendar was instituted. The Gregorian calendar is still in use today[10]

The status of commoner gave Michael the right to be granted property in common with his neighbors. It also meant that Michael became a member of the community of Topsfield. As a member of the community, he would be a church attendee of the Puritan Church. His wife was a member of the Church.[11] I have yet to see a record that indicates that Michael, Sr., became a member of the Church. It was typical for the wife to be a Church member but not necessarily the husband. It was mandatory to attend the required services, so to that extent Michael was an active member. It would not be unusual for a man to only meet this minimum requirement.

As well as being an active participant in the Church, Michael's status as a commoner allowed Michael to hold substantial parcels of land. In addition to his right to land as a commoner as explained below, Michael may have received substantial grants of land from King Charles II of England.[12] This land-grant assumption appears to be based on the theory that Michael was a Huguenot supported by the English king.

The Massachusetts Bay Colony could be likened to a joint-stock company. As such, it was similar to a forerunner of our modern-day corporation. The law indicated that settlers of the Colony who invested in the joint-stock company as limited-liability investors were allotted 200 acres of land for each fifty English pounds invested. Also, each person who came to the Colony at his own expense was to be allotted 50 acres of land for each member of his family.[13] At the time Michael was made a commoner, he was married and had four children.[14]

Michael had purchased land in 1672 upon which he built his house.[15] Eight years in temporary quarters must have been a hardship for Michael and his family. Most observers indicate that Michael arrived in Topsfield in 1664. If he built his house in 1672, this would mean that Michael and his family would be without a permanent home for eight years. As we shall see, this condition may have presented a problem for Michael and his family. There are some who say that

Michael acquired land in 1660.[16] If this condition is true, the time of his temporary existence is even longer.

Mikal may have been a voluntary servant with rudimentary housing. As we pursue the possibility of his indentured servitude to an English lieutenant, we will see that he may have received a small plot of land with a home in the 1660 deed suggested above.

Today, more than 335 years later, his descendents live on parcels of land on Salem Road in Topsfield, Massachusetts, that originated from the original grants and purchases of Michael. The Dwinell family who lives on Salem Road today is descendant of Jacob Dwinell who is a son of Michael Dwinell, Sr.[17]

Michael's wife, Mary, and Michael had their first child, named Mary, in 1668.[18] I have no records of where they lived as a family until Michael's initial creation of the home on Salem Road. As stated earlier, there are some reasonable conjectures. This fact would be important given living conditions in Colonial America in the 1600s.

Before we describe Michael's environment, we need to talk about his possible European origin. As you will soon see, there are several credible but inconclusive theories for us to consider. We should explore each theory before we talk about the Topsfield environment. If we know more about Michael's European origin, we would know more about the environment he faced when he came to Topsfield and his possible reaction.

Many observers indicate that Michael was a French Huguenot. As of this writing, Michael's French origin has not been proven. As my research and the research of others evolve, it is hoped that Michael's origin could be ascertained with a higher degree of certainty.

The national origin of Michael Dwinell, Senior, is a mystery. This mystery will remain until the ship that transported him across the Atlantic Ocean is revealed or until there is some evidence uncovered that proves that he was born in America. Although there is a lack of irrefutable evidence, there is no lack of theories as to the national origin of Michael Dwinell, Senior.

There appears to be a Norman thread holding some of these several theories together, so we should begin with the oldest theory in terms of antiquity. This theory has a strong Norman connection.

My first cousin, Lane Dwinell, gave me some correspondence that links our Dwinell lineage to a Count Do en el from the Normandy province of France. A man named Merrill M. Dwinell of Evanston, Illinois, is responsible for this research. His research reveals a list of rent payers in a community near Liseaux, France. He also has found a Coat of Arms for the Do en el clan dated 1694. He contended that Coats of Arms were to be recorded as ordered by Louis XIV as part of a general registration of nobility.[19] These findings are valuable, but more evidence is needed to show a tie to Michael of Topsfield in America.

There is a degree of logic to the recording of nobility in France in 1694. In the mid 1690s, Louis XIV of France had been in complete power for more than thirty years. Since the death of Jean Baptiste Colbert in 1683, Louis XIV needed to rule by means of his own style. Unlike his early reign when he was so reliant on Cardinal Richeleau or the years when he had the loyal advice of Colbert, he had assumed complete control of the government. The loss of Colbert meant that he lacked the loyal economic and political advice that he needed. Louis XIV needed his nobility to help and advise him.

The excesses of war and expenses at the palace at Versailles were a steady drain on the treasury. King Louis attempted to rule the merchant and peasant classes virtually alone. This condition may explain why King Louis XIV wanted to register the nobility of France. The reign of the king was coming to an end. The extension of commitments had increased dramatically and he needed his allies to help him.[20]

As previously mentioned Frank Dwinell also contends the Count connection. Frank Dwinell ties the Dwinell heritage to the House of Lancaster of England. His research has led Frank Dwinell to think that a Count Do en el accompanied William the Conqueror on his invasion of England in 1066.[21]

After the Norman Invasion, Frank Dwinell contends that the Count received vast land holdings in Scotland, Ireland and England that were presented to his descendents. Although many of the Count's descendents are said to have left England, those who remained are identified with the House of Lancaster. The name of Do en el had been changed to Dunnell as the centuries passed.

It is a matter of record that in 1635 a man named Henry Dunnell sailed on the Bonaventure for the Virginia Colony. Perhaps Michael Dwinell, Senior, may well be the son of Henry Dunnell of the Virginia Colony. Michael Dwinell, Senior, is sometimes referred to as Michael Dunnell. This theory would provide some research problems. I have found references to a Henry Daniel in Virginia at about the same date.[22] It would be common for the surname to have changed. However, when this person would have migrated to New England, what name would he have used?

These companion theories suggest a French origin in the eleventh century. Both theories contend that the French Count came to England on a military adventure. Merrill Dwinell suggests that some of the Count's descendents could have migrated to Scotland or Ireland and that some descendents could have stayed in England or in France.

I had the opportunity to hear a speaker who suggested the use of probability statistics to the determination of the relative reliability of a genealogical contention. He maintained that if you were 95% certain that a relationship of four generations ago, you could state with a less than .95 certainty that the relationship holds to a generation of people today presumably of the same ancestry. The probability would in fact be $(.95(.95(.95(.95) =. 81$[23]

When you consider that Michael Dwinell, Senior, may have been the descendent of this count from the 12th century, you are dealing with about eleven generations from the 12th to the 17th centuries with an additional eleven generations to the present. Added to this probability problem is the existence of the Plague in the 14th century. The probability would be very small, yet, nevertheless, possible. Ignoring the Plague's effect and assuming a .75 confidence in the Count theory, the probability would be P=.75 raised to the 22nd power which would equal P=.0018—obviously a highly unlikely possibility.

We should pursue the Irish contention as well. There are researchers who say that Michael Dwinell came from Ireland, perhaps as early as 1654. This contention has Michael sailing on a ship named the Good Fellow from Kinsale, the port city of Cork, Ireland.[24]

It is a matter of historical record that the systematic settlement of Ireland by the British in the era of Oliver Cromwell caused the displacement of families. Men were sent to the area known as Connaught, beyond the Shannon River. Women were sent to the West Indies and children who were about thirteen or fourteen were placed in indentured servitude in the American Colonies.[25]

There are records of a ship called the Good Fellow with George Dell as its Master. There is a specific tie to the Cromwellian Settlement of Ireland and the Good Fellow. There are various spellings of the surname of the Good Fellow's master. The most common are Dell, Delle and Dill. The endnotes will reveal this variety.

Those who have subscribed to the theory of a Mikal Donnell coming to America as an indentured servant indicate that his master was an English Lieutenant named Samuel Appleton.[26] The theory of Michael Dwinell being an indentured servant to Lieutenant Appleton would need more specific proof.

There is a notation in the Essex County Court records that indicates that Michael was cited for failing to attend Sunday services in April, 1657, as required by law. The court document reads "Michael the Irishman." No last name is provided.[27]

The theory that Michael Dwinell, Senior, was Irish is supported by his great grandson, Solomon, who indicated in his diary that Solomon's grandfather, Michael, had so indicated.[28] Also, there is some evidence that a Mikall Dwoinell possessed a farm in Topsfield as early as 1660.[29]

The concept that Michael Dwinell is Irish suggests that the name be derived from McDonnell or O'Donnell, common Irish names. There is a close connection among the names Donnell, Dunnell and Donel and the many more variations of the name. The descendents of the Count could have migrated to Ireland as both Merrill and Frank Dwinell suggests. If this were the case, they would have had upwards of more than 400 years to be assimilated to the Irish culture.

There were Irish youth placed into indentured servitude in the Massachusetts Bay Colony. As we pursue the Irish contention, we should consider their story. Let us consider the plight of these Irish youth as we consider the possibility of Michael being Irish and but one of the hundreds of Irish youth "Shanghaied" into indentured servitude in America.

Someplace in Ireland in late 1653, perhaps in County Cork on the outskirts of the city of Cork, a thirteen or fourteen year old boy was wandering the streets. His parents had been separated from him rather systematically through the implementation of the specific mandates of Oliver Cromwell. This boy was but one of a group of homeless and parentless children left to fend for themselves.

There is a Thomas Donnell, age 44 in 1653, who was "relocated" to Connaught, a region to the west of the Shannon River and east of the Atlantic Ocean.[30] The origin of this Thomas Donnell was in an area near the city of Cork. Thomas is a prominent given name through the first four generations of the Dwinell family in America. Is this a coincidence?

Thomas' banishment to this region was not his alone. Many of his countrymen were sent to the west of Ireland or sent to Spain to fight England's war. In many instances families were shattered as wives were sent to the Caribbean Islands to comfort the British soldiers. Hence, the abandonment of the children left to wander the streets.

England had planned the resettlement of a part of Ireland that can be described by forming a triangle with a line drawn from Dublin to the northeast to Cork in the southwest. The southeast coast of Ireland formed the triangle's base, and the Irish Sea coast back to Dublin was its third side. This area was to be cleared to replicate an English settlement. The indigent Irish needed to be removed.

This circumscribed sector was referred to as the Pale. The Irish, one way or another, were "transplanted" beyond the Pale. The expression "Beyond the Pale" has various meanings today suggesting beyond the usual explanation. In this case, quite literally, people were removed beyond their original region of residence.

The third part of this diabolical political adventure was the systematic deportation of the Irish children into indentured servitude in the American colonies. The Irish theory of the European origin of Michael Dwinell is that one of these children was the thirteen or fourteen year-old boy named Mikal Donnell. The resultant 3,500-mile trek across the Atlantic in a slave ship gave the expression "Beyond the Pale" a new meaning.

The story of this political adventure, as it relates to young Mikal, begins in the city of Boston of the Massachusetts Bay Colony. Several business persons in Boston were to establish ownership of a ship named the Good Fellow.[31] Two of these businesspersons were George Delle and Richard Leader. George Delle would become the Master of the Good Fellow. Richard Leader would emerge as a businessman who would work with his partner, David Sellick, systematically to kidnap Irish "vagabonds" off the streets of Ireland. These incorrigible vagabonds were orphaned by Cromwell's edicts. The circuitous reasoning that placed this pejorative label on these youth provides a graphic example of the diabolical nature of Cromwell's plan.[32]

As Delle and Leader were acquiring their boat in Boston, political activity in London, England and Dublin, Ireland, was creating the governmental decrees needed for Delle, Leader and Sellick to negotiate their nefarious enterprise. A chronology of the specific governmental directives shown in the endnotes provides the reader with a sense of the inevitable plight of these poor children including Mikal. In early 1654, Mikal may have been one of the 400 children who sailed out of the port of Kinsale, Ireland, on a 3,500-mile, four-month journey to another continent.[33]

Several researchers contend that Mikal emerged in America as the indentured servant of Lieutenant Samuel Appleton in Ipswich of the Massachusetts Bay Colony.[34] There is historical evidence that George Delle, the Good Fellow Master, sold children into indentured servitude.[35] Although a bill of sale for Mikal has not been revealed as yet, there is some evidence that he may have worked in servitude.

The tax records of Topsfield for 1668 indicate that he owed a tax bill to support the local minister of 5 shillings, 6 pence. A man named Anthony Carroll owed exactly the same amount.[36] It is believed that Carroll was a former indentured servant who sailed on the Good Fellow in 1654. It was a common practice for a master to provide a home for his servant at the end of the required term of servitude. The similarity of the amount of the tax bill for Donnell and Carroll appears more than a coincidence.

Mikal was a witness in defense of Carroll in 1667. A man named Patteson was suing Carroll for defamation of character. The remedy that Patteson was seeking was Carroll's house and land. The nature of the testimony revealed that Carroll was an indentured servant. As previously mentioned, a servant of Appleton named "Michael the Irishman" was cited in Court for not attending religious services on a Sunday in 1657. Some researchers think that this Michael was Mikal Donnell.

There is further evidence that my ancestor, Mikal, may be Irish. My search for absolute conclusive evidence has revealed some new evidence. Recently, I answered a request from the National Genographic Project to be a participant.

The results indicated that I belong to the Y chromosome r1b (M343) haplogroup. This genetic grouping indicates that I am of Celtic origin. Further investigation of this haplogroup by the Genograpic Project indicates that about 98% of men from northwestern Ireland belong to this haplogroup.[37] This is the specific area of Ireland to which men were exiled during the Cromwellian Settlement. It is boarded by the Atlantic Ocean to the west and the Shannon River to the east. Thus, the inhabitants could be controlled.

Irish myth supported by history tells tales of the invasion of the Milesians from Spain in about 1,000 B.C.[38] These Milesian people together with other Irish tribes form the Celtic and Gaelic people who are typically Irish. Donnell is an Irish Gaelic name. These Irish people were typically Roman Catholic.

Young Michael wandering the streets of Ireland trying to survive perhaps did not have the opportunity to contemplate his religion. Mikal became Anglicized in servitude and then as a resident of this Puritan environment. Then, his surname and religious identity would change. The English were good at the arts of identity changes and forced servitude of its colonists.

There were many servants living in the Massachusetts Bay Colony during the seventeenth into the eighteenth century. In fact one researcher states that there were more servants than there were non-servant persons in the Massachusetts Bay Colony.

A servant was defined as a person who provided services to another person. Many of these servants provided services for compensation. Also, many servants were not compensated.[40]

Of the servants who were not compensated there were voluntary and non-voluntary servants who were provided only room and board. Typically, colonists who experienced voluntary servitude agreed to a term of four to seven years of indenture as payment for passage from Europe to America.[41]

Involuntary servants included black slaves, English prisoners, indebted persons working off money owed and Irish and Scotch youth "transplanted" to the American colonies.

Typically, voluntary and involuntary indentured servants who were living with their masters were not compensated during their term of service. Often, at the end of their indenture, they may be kept by their former master to be paid at the going rate for their level of skill as a service provider. An unskilled person would be paid two shillings a week.

It was the custom to provide a set of tools and a suit of clothes to the servant at the end of his or her servitude. Some masters provided a house and a plot of land. Some researchers, principally John Quigley, state that Mikal received land and shelter at the end of his servitude.

Mikal may have continued to work as a voluntary servant for Lieutenant Appleton. The farm community of Topsfield was essentially a barter economy. At two shillings a week Mikal could barely have saved the 50 pounds needed to make the real estate purchase in 1672, but it would have been possible. It should be noted that servants were on call to their employers for 24 hours per day. Forced savings in these circumstances was a strong likelihood.

It has been stated that there is a 1660 deed indicating that Mikal acquired property in Topsfield. This deed has not yet been revealed to me, although the 1667 tax bill was against some legal source indicating land ownership. The last bit of evidence that reveals an Irish country of origin is the name on the 1672 deed that represents original ownership of the family homestead in Topsfield that has survived all these centuries. The grantee on this real estate deed is Mikal Donnell. Donnell is generally recognized as an Irish surname,

The last and most oft repeated theory is that Michael was a French Huguenot who escaped religious persecution. It is contended that he was a wealthy person and was given grants of land in Essex County by King Charles II of England. The concept of the grants from King Charles II appears to be the consensus point of view of the Topsfield Historical Society.[42] The lack of an existence of a passenger list still remains the problem barring this researcher from dogmatically stating that this or any other theory is valid.

It should be noted that it is difficult to obtain passenger lists for ships sailing after 1635. One reason for this difficulty is that passengers were measured more as cargo than specific individuals.

The contention that Michael Dwinell was related to Count Do en el appears to have rather thin support. It would take considerable research to verify the opinions of Merrill and Frank Dwinell. The intervening centuries from the Count in the 12th century to Michael in the 17th century have revealed little or no evidence of the sustaining of the family line. The information received from Merrill Dwinell is interesting, but the dates are off. Those researchers who claim a French connection claim that Michael came to America in the mid 1660s. The disclosure of Merrill Dwinell's research refers to the Dwinell family in France in more recent history.

The possibility of Michael being Irish appears more credible. The passage of centuries belies a connection to the House of Lancaster. The possibility of a tie to an O'Donnell clan is feasible. There were indentured slaves from Ireland and the evidence of Michael Donnell's indenture to Lieutenant Samuel Appleton appears credible.

The Huguenot connection from France through England to America appears reasonably feasible. The connection to King Charles II needs to be researched more carefully to support a tie. Apparently, Michael did have funds and a degree of influence when he arrived in Topsfield. It would appear that there is at least some circumstantial evidence that points to the Huguenot and King Charles II connection.

As stated earlier, all of these versions are moot until Michael's name appears on a passenger list or some other official document that reveals his passage to America or trip from Virginia. We do know that Michael Dwinell, Senior, was a man of some wealth who appeared in Topsfield in the Massachusetts Bay Colony in 1664 or some years before. From this generation on the narrative of Michael, Senior, and his descendents can be verified with more credibility.

Without prejudice to other theories, I intend to proceed with the assumption that Michael was Irish. Recently, this appears to have become the most accepted theory, so the thread of the story would be aided by this contention. As we go along, some of our sources are based on the Huguenot contention as well as the Irish contention. Although this duality may cause some confusion, a discussion of both probabilities would enhance the understanding of this era.[43]

The Huguenot religion appears to be a branch of Calvinism and has a tie to the Puritan Church, the state church of the Massachusetts Bay Colony. The Huguenot faith's origins are in the Roman Catholic country of France.

Huguenots suffered religious persecution in France at this point in history. As a result, it was not uncommon for Huguenots to migrate from country to country. Although Michael may have been born in France, he may have lived in one or more other countries before arriving in America.

French Huguenots were able to escape from their native country. There were many routes, several of which went through England. In a mercantilist world, England would be happy to accept refugees from adversarial nations.

As a forerunner to capitalism, mercantilism was an economic system that supported the aims of the mother country. Population played a role. England was still an agrarian society in the 17th century. An increase in population would help England while a decrease in population would hurt France.

Except for the royalty connection, it is not clear why King Charles II of England would fund Michael's adventure in America. Michael did appear to have funds to purchase land beyond his grant as a commoner. Also, if he were not an indentured slave, he had to pay for his voyage. These conditions add to the mystery of the European origin of this man.

His decision to come to America must have been made early in life. By some accounts, Michael was 24 years of age when he arrived in Topsfield in 1664. Other accounts have him in Topsfield at age 20 in 1660.

The Irish contention would have Michael arriving on the slave ship Good Fellow in 1654. Then, Michael would have upwards of seven years of indentured servitude to face. Perhaps Lieutenant Appleton would be influential in getting Michael started in nearby Topsfield.

In most of these scenarios as to the European origin of Michael, an ocean voyage would have been necessary. Since we haven't identified his boat with certainty, we should explore what passenger voyages across the North Atlantic would be like in the seventeenth century. An account of these voyages would help us understand the life experiences of the residents of Puritan Massachusetts.

A modern non-fiction book entitled *The Perfect Storm* by Sebastian Junger points out the perils of the North Atlantic Ocean.[44] The Andrea Gail was the ship fated to sink in the North Atlantic Ocean in 1991 as depicted by Junger.

This ship was a modern sword boat. The crew had very thorough charts of the Atlantic Ocean, a very competent Coast Guard presence of two nations, sophisticated audio communication and expert twenty-four hour weather information. Their geographic positioning system equipment allowed them to know where they were on earth within fifty feet.

The Andrea Gail was seventy-two feet long and twenty feet wide. Despite an experienced crew, state of the art equipment and virtually perfect knowledge of the elements and environment, this boat sank. Many boats have met a similar fate in the North Atlantic Ocean. Many of these boats were larger and more powerful than the Andrea Gail.

The architecture of boat construction and the physics of ocean wave action explain the dangers of the sea. A boat's captain may find himself climbing a wave higher than the boat's length thereby be capsized, or be rolled over by a wave higher than the boat's width. Even the most modern marine technology can't combat these natural elements.

If we relate this modern-day example to the experience of the seventeenth century, we might imagine the concerns of these pioneers. Ted Morgan in his book *Wilderness at Dawn* places this problem in an interesting context. "It took Captain Newport more than four months to sail his three ships—the Susan Constant, the Godspeed and the Discovery—to the shores of Virginia with their 105 passengers. The Discovery, a two-masted pinnace, was hardly more than a thirty-five foot rowboat with sails. Yet, it carried twenty-one men plus enough food and water for the trip. In today's terms, imagine a four-month ride in an ocean-going subway car at rush hour."[45]

I own an eighteen and one-half foot motor boat that I use on Lake Winnepesaukee, a substantial New Hampshire lake. The largest expanse on this lake is twenty-six miles. Yet, when the wind is greater than 10–15 miles per hour, I have difficulty navigating these waters. I must admit that at my best I was far from an expert mariner.

The North Atlantic Ocean has an expanse of thousands of miles for more wave action to be developed and sustained. Imagine the recurring winds and wave action over these four months of Captain Newport and his passengers' experience.

The Mayflower was a larger boat, 96 feet long by 25 feet wide. The cramped living quarters housed about 100 people. One crew member aboard the replica of the Mayflower in Plymouth, Massachusetts, harbor has said "Think of it as a cottage where a hundred people are always home." The trip took sixty-seven days.[46]

It is reasonable to relate these experiences to the plight of the Cuban defectors trying to reach Florida. These "boats" used by Cuban defectors are mere rafts for the most part. The conditions are worse; the distance is shorter. The Bonaventure that brought Henry Dunnell to Virginia in 1635 had 100 passengers.[47] I do not know the dimensions of this ship. The reader will recall the mention of the Bonaventure voyage in support of the English European origin of Michael.

There was another problem. The captains of these early ships were sailing in uncharted waters. Although one's latitude could be determined, the determination of longitude was another matter. The determination of longitude with reliable certainty would not be possible for more than 100 years after Michael's 1600s voyage.[48]

Imagine approaching the coasts of Newfoundland, Nova Scotia or Maine knowing where you were only with a certainty within 150 miles. This technical limitation added even more peril to the voyage. Yet families came across this ocean.

The Massachusetts Bay Colony was an English colony, so the ships, for the most part, were English. It was important for England to colonize America. These voyages were a major part of the power-political policy of the mother country—so the pioneers came.

Both Spain and France invested in explorations in the sixteenth century. As a result, each country held vast geographic domains in the New World. The French developed control of the inland sectors of much of what are now Canada and the United States. This control would prove to be a threat to the Massachusetts Bay Colony. Spain and France as well as Holland were adversaries to England, and often to each other.

Spain in the southern part of what is now called the United States and in Latin America was in search of gold and other riches. France relied on the fur trade to a large extent. England chose to colonize the eastern coast of North America.

France and England were bitter rivals for control of the New World. England was ready to accept Frenchmen fleeing their country for religious reasons. The political climate that Michael faced as he reached Topsfield would soon embroil several of his descendants in the Colonial Wars, familiarly known as the French and Indian Wars.

The colonists of the Massachusettss Bay Colony were like pawns in a huge international chess game. The English were competing with the Dutch and Portugal for trade opportunities in the Far East of Asia. The English, French and Spanish were competing for naval control of the western coast of Europe.

While the English settled on the eastern shores of America, they were in competition with the Dutch who controlled what is now southern New York State. The French controlled a vast territory of inland America ranging from southern Canada to some of the southern parts of what we know as the United States, particularly the Mississippi River area. The French also controlled the Great Lakes and the St. Lawrence River. The Spanish controlled the area we now call Latin America and much of the southern and southwestern parts of the current United States.

We learn as school children that St. Augustine, Florida, is the oldest community in the United States. The story of Ponce De Leon and the Spanish is interesting. It is a less well-known fact that Fort Michilimackinac in Northern Michigan is the second oldest community. The fort was a French outpost.

The English chose to colonize their territory as the Spanish chose to explore, conquer and pillage. Meanwhile, the French chose to use their military to manipulate the Indians for military purposes as they engaged in trade with the Indian populations. As we shall see, the English model emerged successfully. It should be noted that the English certainly tried to use military clout to manipulate the Indians. The French were better at this art.[49] It should also be noted that the Spanish acted, as a matter of strategy, to acquire gold and precious jewelry while the French and English used trade in various forms as a mode of mercantilist economic strategy.[50] None of the three countries should feel more proud of their humane behavior than their competition.

The English strategy created considerable hardships for the colonists, since the inhabitants of the North American English colonies bore the brunt of the wars of the seventeenth and eighteenth centuries that raged across this newly discovered continent. Dwinell family members who are descendants of Michael became embroiled in the Colonial Wars during the eighteenth century. The Colonial Wars is the official name for what is now familiarly known as the French and Indian Wars. In fact, one of the Colonial Wars is the French and Indian War. Michael's grandson, Benjamin, would play a role in the French and Indian War as would other grandsons of Michael, Senior.

Beyond these rivalries, principally with France, the Dwinell family also became embroiled in the Revolutionary War. Thus, descendants of Michael Dwinell, Senior, are descendants of both the Colonial and the Revolutionary Wars.

Given this animosity between France and England, you can see the problem of this adventuresome young man who found himself essentially alone in an English community, on the frontier of a new land amongst people of another religion and native of another country. Yet, he was accepted into this community and appeared to have prospered. We should look at what life was like for Michael, his wife, Mary, and their rather substantial family of nine children.

With the one exception of Michael's remarkable rose bushes, there appears to be nothing uncommon about the original Dwinell house on Old Salem Road in Topsfield. I might add, though, that Michael appeared to have money. He has been described by one source as "the not poor, but honest yeoman of Topsfield, Essex County, Massachusetts."[51] We should assume that he husbanded that money carefully and lived as other settlers would have lived.

We have noted that it appears that Michael arrived in Topsfield alone to serve out his servitude with Lieutenant Appleton. There appears to be no evidence that he lived with any of the townspeople after his servitude and before his marriage to Mary, so I assume he created his own environment. Taking a person in as a semi-permanent guest would be a problem as our description of typical Colonial housing of the mid-seventeenth century will soon indicate.

Even today, more than 335 years later, Topsfield, Massachusetts is a rural community. I have driven to Topsfield often since beginning the project of creating this book. My usual route is to arrive from the south on United States Route 1. The drive through Saugus and Danvers, Massachusetts, is past many commercial enterprises. It is easy to realize that you are driving on the outskirts of the major American city of Boston. Then, the Topsfield town line appears and one is suddenly in the country. The terrain in the southeast sector of Topsfield appears to have changed little over the centuries. It is always easy for me to imagine the environment facing Michael, since this is the part of town that Michael owned.

One can only imagine how rural this small town was in 1664, or 1660, when Michael arrived in Topsfield. To give you an idea, in 1661, there were 30 commoners in the town. Imagine the geographic size of your city or town and, then, imagine only 30 families on this piece of geography.[52] There was some community life, since the town began to be established in 1639–41.[53] It would be reasonable to assume that a main street existed in the center of town. However, the outskirts of town would be another matter. In colonial times roads had a habit of ending a few yards out of the center of town. The area of Michael's home is about one mile from the center of town on Salem Road. Eventually, Salem Road was to become a connecting road to Salem Village, the current-day Danvers.

How would Michael live; what kind of housing would he have? If Lieutenant Appleton did not provide Michael with a house, he would have had a problem. Topsfield is quite hilly, so he could literally have built a dugout into the side of a hill as many colonists did before they built their home. He could also erect an English teepee, a reasonable facsimile of the Indian counterpart. These rudimentary structures would present a daunting experience during northeastern Massachusetts winters, particularly with a wife and children, but these choices would not be uncommon.[54] Michael had married Mary in 1668 and had two children prior to purchasing a large plot of land on Salem Road.

Michael needed to clear the land for subsistence farming in order to survive. Clearing land is always hard work. Let's explore the nature of the task confronting Michael. Even though the community of Topsfield was nearby, Michael would have been confronted with the Great American Forest.

Let's see if we can get a sense of what this man was facing. Think of the largest tree in your town.[55] Go to where it grows to get a sense of how tall and wide it is. Now, imagine this tree as only one tree among millions in a dense forest reaching from northern Canada to the Gulf of Mexico and from the Atlantic Ocean to the Mississippi River.[56] Actually, these big trees in communities are called trophy trees[57]-forestry experts call them witness trees.[58] In the forest, trees had to vie for survival with other trees. These trees would survive by growing toward the sun. The trees may be prevented from being as wide as trophy or witness trees of the same type but may in fact be taller. Forest density has its effect on the trees of the forest.[59]

To say this forest was dense tells only part of the story. In fact, with little exception, the foliage from these trees blocked the sun. It would be difficult to see the top of a given tree from the ground. To place this environment in perspective, some observers have noted that a squirrel could climb a tree at the Atlantic Ocean coast and, then, never touch ground again until it reached the Mississippi River.[60]

There is another sense I can provide. Ten years prior to Michael's experience, in 1654, a farmer in Concord, Massachusetts, ventured into his land to work. Then, he went into his own wood lot and became lost such was the density of the forest.[61] This condition existed in the eastern portion of North America when the colonists came to this continent in the 1600s. The Vikings had come to North America several centuries before the English and French. The Vikings did not choose to colonize their discoveries on a large or permanent scale here, so their presence proved to have little effect on the North American environment.[62]

The Vikings have had an effect upon the Dwinell experience. Some of the theories I have mentioned regarding Michael's national origin have a Norman, therefore, Viking influence. The Vikings at one point in history controlled a large part of Europe and part of Asia. Specific to our conjectures, the Vikings controlled much of Scotland, Ireland and England as well as Normandy, France. Thus, a common thread through the various theories about the Dwinell national origin is a Viking, or Norman influence.[63]

It is true that the Indians had been on this continent before the colonists. In fact, these Indians had lived in North America for 15,000 years or longer according to most historians. They lived along the seashore and along the shores of lakes, rivers, and streams. North America was very sparsely populated when the colonists came to America.

The Indians ventured into the dense forests only to hunt or to move, as they often did. There were Indian trails for these purposes, but Indians traveled much more lightly than the European originated white people did. In his History of Topsfield, Mass., George Francis Dow provides a sense of an Indian trail as he quotes the town clerk of Woburn writing in 1654. "the Indian paths being not above one foot broad, so that a man may travell many days and never find one.... In travelling through unknowne woods, and through watery swamps, they (the settlers) discovr the fittness of the place, sometimes passing through the thicketts...."[64]

Other than this activity, the forests were left uninterrupted to grow for 20,000 years as the glaciers receded after the Ice Age until the white man came to create their civilization growing to the society we know today. Remember, also, that the Indians were still in the Stone Age. Their tools were fashioned from stone, not iron or steel. They hardly had the capacity to fell a giant tree or to clear a forest in a European's sense of the term.[65]

What did the existence of this forest mean to Michael and his fellow colonists as they confronted the problem before them? Topsfield is near the Atlantic Ocean, and the Ipswich River that runs through it is a substantial stream. There is evidence that Indians may have lived along this river.[66] It is reasonable to assume that the people who came to Topsfield before Michael developed the optimal land. Topsfield was organized as a community beginning in 1639. In fact, it was typical for the colonist to inhabit land just recently abandoned by the Indians, sometimes living in Indian quarters and utilizing the cleared land until they created a more typical European-type environment. It is reasonable to assume that Michael did not have this luxury. The residents who arrived before him would have laid claim to this former Indian-owned and cleared land.[67]

Since Topsfield is about five miles inland from the ocean, the forest density was a problem confronting Michael. Even today, the second-growth trees of Topsfield are impressive. Michael had the community nearby, and he may have made some early friends, but he had the enormous task of clearing his land. Now, let us get a little more specific as to the nature of this land given the presence of the forest. Think of a given year of weather in New England. Sometime between January and March we can expect a major blizzard with heavy gales or even hurricane-style winds. These winds together with icing would cause large branches or even trees to fall. The late spring and summer bring a few violent thunder and lightening storm, squalls from line storms or even a rare tornado.

Hurricane season is from August to October. In late fall Nor'easters attack our trees. Imagine these conditions prevailing for 20,000 years with virtually no cleanup after storms. Also, think of the life of a tree. The varieties of trees in northeastern Massachusetts range in maximum age from a little older than 100 years to about 370 years.[68] How many trees grew, matured, died and fell over this 20,000 year span? Imagine the task before the colonists as they viewed this dark, cluttered forest. To be specific, there was a hurricane in 1635. Both Increase and Cotton Mather describes the felling of thousands of trees in this storm.[69] Imagine the chaos! The 1938 hurricane attacked a pre settlement forest called the old-growth Pisgah forest in an area near Rindge, New Hampshire south of Keene, New Hampshire. Accounts of the devastation indicate what a colonist would have been up against in Topsfield after the 1635 hurricane.[70]

The Indians may have helped with the clearing of some of this debris. Where they lived, Indians would burn the forest floor. If you view a substantial second-growth forest today, there are two obvious characteristics. First, the over top or canopy of the forest is somewhat uniform since trees in the previously cleared forest started to grow back at the same time. Second, the floor of the forest is characterized as having considerable debris. Indians who populated the forest prior to colonization may have cleared the forest floor to some extent.

The task of clearing a forest of this magnitude would be daunting for us today even with bulldozers, chain saws and tractors and other modern equipment. There were virtually no forests in Europe save for Scandinavia and part of Germany. The English colonists were accustomed to a way of life that did not include large forests with which to cope.[71]

Before the colonists fashioned better tools, they were faced with a dense and dangerous forest that had to be cleared to let in the sun and to create a settlement similar to the life they knew in Europe. The Indians provided some help but, mostly, the colonist was left alone to carve out a civilization.

One can imagine Michael clearing a small plot. First, he had to cut down some trees. However, he couldn't see high enough to know if there were already fallen huge branches and actual trees held up only by the tree being cut. These fallen trees and branches were dangerous weapons that could come down upon him if he were not careful. Many colonists died from fallen timber.[72] Modern-day forestry experts provide an explanation of this dangerous condition. In an old-growth-pre-European settlement forest, there are a variety of types of trees. Some tall trees act as a canopy for the shorter trees of another type. In this case, it would be difficult to see what existed beyond a given height of forest.[73]

An example of an old-growth forest is on the Indian Trail of Mount Wachusett in Princeton, Massachusetts. This forest gives one a good sense of density and debris. However, the height of the mountain as it stands alone in the Central Massachusetts environment makes this forest vulnerable to severe weather. There is virtually no canopy to this forest and the trees are not as large as they would be in a protected area.[74]

There are other examples of old-growth-pre-settlement forests in New England in rather remote and mountainous areas. The references provided would give you an idea where to look.[75] Michael may have learned a trick or two from the Indians.

The Indians had a solution. They girdled trees.[76] The girdling process was the cutting of a small, circular ridge around the circumference of the tree to the quick. The quick is the wood directly beneath the bark. Once this portion of the tree is cut, the tree will die as a season passes. Then, the leaves will not grow and the sun will enter. Crops will then grow. For a typical European, this was a slow process. One has to believe that Michael had the same reaction.

Michael did survive, though, and his life progressed. Let's explore the contribution he made to the Town of Topsfield and to the Dwinell heritage. First, let us look at the housing that Michael Dwinell would have developed for his family. Thus, we can better understand life in the Massachusetts Bay Colony.

There are two examples of housing that would give us some idea of the environment Michael could have created. The Peak House[77] on the outskirts of Medfield, Massachusetts, is a good example of Colonial housing of this era. Also, the Plimouth Plantation in Plymouth, Massachusetts, is another example.[78] There are other examples of Colonial housing. If you are interested in pursuing this topic, be sure to view housing of the 1600s as typical examples.

Typically, Colonial housing was expanded.[79] This expansion was usually outward on the first floor to the other side of the fireplace. The fireplace usually was in one corner of the room when the house was first built. An expansion would place the fireplace in the center of the room.[80]

These modern-day examples are somewhat inadvertently romanticized. They are replicas of colonial architecture, but they have been well preserved. Their size is reasonably accurate, but the initial construction would have been somewhat more rudimentary.

There was plenty of wood to create housing but remember the inexperience of these settlers. For the most part, these pioneers led simple lives in their native land. They did not own land.[81] So, they hardly had the tools for the task confronting them. They had lived in simple huts in England, and for Michael, possibly in Ireland or France.

Even when the settlers were to create more permanent homes, the clapboards created would have been uneven and rough-hewn. The caulking would have been mud. Both of these conditions would have created a porous, drafty interior.[82]

Sometime in late November, the first snowfall occurs. We, who live in Massachusetts, welcome the first snow. It is pretty and somehow, the air seems crisper and cleaner. After a hot summer, we look forward to the coolness to follow—but not the severe cold, high winds and blizzards.

The colonists were resourceful, though. In the established towns better structures would soon follow. The Peak House appears to be a building that would not be added to easily. This house has a severely pitched roof to allow snow to slide off. It is a two-story building with a loft quite similar to an "A" frame house of today. Think of a small summer cottage at a lake or at the beach.

The space in this type of house is adequate for two adults in the summer. It could even be satisfactory for a teenage family as they and their friends slept on cots or sleeping bags on the floor. It would be a challenge to stay there in the winter, though, and most families have not set up a permanent home in this type of cottage. This typical summer cottage would be about the size of the Peak House or a house in the Plimouth Plantation. Imagine a family of nine children and two parents living is this type of accommodation all winter. This condition gives a new definition to "cabin fever."

One reliable observer recounts that the Plimouth Plantation is an accurate replica of life at Plymouth seven years after the Pilgrims landed.[83] The Peak House is represented as a typical house of the era.

The houses at Plimouth can be more easily added to and perhaps this is what Michael did as his family grew. He and his wife, Mary, had nine children. They had four children when first granted land. So, even then, they had a substantial housing problem. When you visit one of these replicas of homes of our early settlers, don't be alarmed by the shortness of the thresholds or the ceilings. People were quite short, then, as we can assume Michael was.[84] The houses were small as well, and one wonders how a family of eleven could have lived there. This large family was not uncommon, at least in the Dwinell experience

Although there were large families, the average family size was low. The reasons for this apparent contradiction were the incidence of childhood disease and the difficulties of child birth. As we shall see in a subsequent chapter, the English did not set up a hospital system in the colonies or provide medical expertise.

How did they keep warm? The obvious answer is that they had a fireplace. An efficient fireplace throws off substantial heat. Since heat rises, the loft would be cozy. But, what happens at night? Herein lays a problem.

The man of the house, typically, had the task of banking the fire. He had to be careful. If he let the embers go too low, the fire would go out and the family would be in danger of freezing to death in the northeastern Massachusetts cold. If he let the embers flame too high, the house could burn to the ground endangering the inhabitants. Both the loss of a fire and the burning of homes occurred all too frequently.[85]

Michael survived as did his family. Although there is no authentic account of his home that I have found, his descendants had substantial homes in Topsfield on his land. At one time his land extended from Middleton, in the west, to Wenham on the eastern edge of the town. Michael became an important member of the community.[86]

The first reference that I have found to Michael's tenure as an active citizen is his appointment as the hog ringer of the town.[87] This duty was more important than you might first suspect.

Early in America there were little or no cattle, either dairy or beef cattle, since there was no grass.[88] Grass could not grow under the cover of the trees. Except for the immediate sea shore the land was almost entirely bereft of grass. This condition made the hog an important source of protein.

Hogs can live without grass. In fact they thrived in the wild. Domestication of the hog was not easy. They tended to roam and become a nuisance. Yet, these same hogs were an important food supply. Michael's task was the enforcement of rules to identify and control the hog population. Together with wild turkeys and other game, the hog was an important food item.

Michael held other offices in the Topsfield community. He gave the Dwinell family a substantial start. His will attests to a more than adequate legacy.[89] This legacy continued. As I have researched the direct line of descent from Michael to our grandchildren, I have found that we are quite widespread across our country. If you doubt that this surname is not widespread, go to www.google.com and enter the name Dwinell and observe the entries that would emerge

Michael gave the Dwinell family its start in America as did other pioneers for their families. Consider the life of Michael given the differing national origins the various theories suggest.

What kind of life would Michael, the Frenchman, have in this essentially English country? Huguenot and Puritan religions were similar, but the English people were quite different from the French as they are today.

Imagine Michael as the descendant of a count. How would he have adapted to rugged frontier life in this unforgiving and unending land? Also, how would he have accepted this egalitarian but harshly religious community?

Michael the native-born American by way of the Virginia Colony would have had a daunting set of experiences for one so young. How did these experiences fashion him?

How would Michael, the Irishman, adapt to being the slave of a British officer? Then, how would he adapt to life in a British colony when he obtained his freedom?

Obviously, whatever his origin and prior experience may have been, he was successful. As we shall see, his descendants have been successful as well as they have contributed, sometimes quite dramatically, to the society that has grown to the country we know today.

Michael Dwinell, Sr., started a clan in America that would grow exponentially as the decades and centuries went by. Michael's children stayed in Topsfield as their father did. They made their mark on the community as well.

Michael and his wife, Mary, would have nine children. They had a long life together. Michael died in 1717 at age 77. There is no information about Mary's exact year of birth or the time that she died. It is known that she was still alive when Michael wrote his will in 1710.[89] Although many women lived to an advanced age, it was common for women to die as a result of pregnancies or to have difficult deliveries. There were large families in many instances, but small families were common, too, due to the problems of bearing children.

Men and women had defined roles in the family and community. Men tended the farm and the wood lot, hunted and maintained the property. Men also played a role in the town government. Women were the leaders of the church. Women ran the home and the nearby area outside of the home. This book is entitled Michael's Roses; it could well be called Mary's Roses. Mary probably initiated and sustained the flower growth.

Life for a woman was lonely, difficult and filled with unending toil. Houses were cold and drafty. In addition to rearing her nine children, Mary had the unending tasks of laundry, cleaning, cooking and tending to the immediate environs of the home. The church was a source of respite and local community and political involvement.

Mary delivered nine children. The oldest child was Mary. Her marriage name was Mary Hovey. The oldest son of Michael, Sr., and Mary Dwinell was Michael Dwinell, Jr. He was born on December 5, 1670, in Topsfield, Massachusetts Bay Colony. As Michael and Mary's children become part of the narrative of Michael, Jr., their role in the family will be discussed.

The next generation, Michael and Mary's grand children, were to begin the exodus to the hinterlands of New England and beyond. Some of Michael, Sr.'s descendants have remained in Topsfield to the current generation. Michael, Sr., and his wife, Mary, had 37 grand children.

2

Michael, Jr., the Doctor

o o o o o o o o o o o o o o o o o o o o o o o o o o o o o o o o o o
"The question of some medical man to serve them was a matter considered deeply by the colonists."

—*Henry Follansbee Long*

Michael Dwinell, Sr.'s oldest son, Michael, is my great, great, great, great, great grand father.[1] I intend to concentrate on Michael's life. I will mention his siblings as they relate to Michael's story. This pattern will follow as I relate the experiences of that portion of the Dwinell clan that descends to the current eleventh generation. This odyssey will begin with the remarkable life of Michael Dwinell, Jr.[2]

As Michael approached adulthood, the town of Topsfield was rapidly becoming an emergent community. The rudimentary shelters experienced by Michael, Sr., and his fellow townsmen had expanded to rather sizable homesteads. Typically, families were large including members of extended families as part of a household.

A good example of the size of homes in the late seventeenth century and early eighteenth century is the Capen House in Topsfield, Massachusetts. This building is a rather large home built for the town minister, Reverend Joseph Capen.[3] A visit to this home would give one a sense of the building that had evolved from the structures created by the early pioneers.

As previously noted, in some cases families were small. In addition to the dangers of childbirth for both mother and child, childhood and adult diseases took their toll. These medical problems would help explain the common incidence of large families yet the small average family sizes of many colonial towns of this era.

The second generation of colonists was still basically English. The first generation pioneers had left a feudal existence in England to form a more egalitarian society. As the end of the seventeenth century loomed, the colonists had apparently made the transition from life on the English countryside to the holders of rather substantial parcels of land.

The experience of this new continent was far different than the life on the tailored and carefully circumscribed towns of England. The ownership of land in Colonial America was less than precise. As Michael, Junior's, generation began their adult life in Topsfield, the lack of preciseness of the perimeter of their land holdings would pose a problem. The best proof of the ownership of land is the deed.

As you read a deed for the typical real estate of today, the language is quite clear. The bounds are set with exact reference for each piece of real property as is the language of the deed of the abutting property. For most of New England today, the property of one entity abuts the property of another entity. For the most part, there is little or no ambiguity.

In colonial times, the typical language of deeds was not totally clear. The expression "more or less" is contained in many early deeds. Also, landmarks are used that could easily be removed as decades went by. These companion ambiguities created land disputes between neighbors and between towns. Michael would be involved in this land problem as one of his community duties. Please note the language of a deed that follows. This deed transferred land to Michael Dwinell, Sr., in 1672."ffrancis Pabody and Mary Pabody to Micail Doniel Sold bargained & warranted for, and in consideration of seventy Pounds, lawful currency, a certain Tract of Land being Devission Land, par whereof that purchased of John How, and part of it purchased of Isaac Comings, as by these several deeds under their hands, and scale doth, and may appear by same Devission—The whole containing by estimation Fifty Acres be it more, or less__Scituate, lyeing & being in Topsfield aforesaid on the South Syde of the River called Ipswich River, being bounded toward the southeast, partly by the Land of Joseph Porter partly by the Land of Mr. William Perkins, and in pt by Salem Line, towards the south East cove, common toward the North & West bounded by the land of Edmond Cooane, and toward the West bounded by the Salem Line—Also the Fifth pt of a piece of meadow purchased of the Towne of Topsfield, also Ten Acres purchased of Isaac Comings yt of the undevided land bounded &c by land of Joseph Porter, Ensign Howlet and by the North east by Wenham meadows Signed and delivered the 24th day of October in the twenty fourth year of the regne of y Soveraigne Lord Charles the Second, by the Grace of God, of Great Britaine, ffraance and Ireland King, defender of the faith et cet Anno Domin 1672...."[4]

The language is the now archaic language of the late seventeenth century. Granted, the people of the day would have interpreted the contemporary spelling, word usage and convention appropriately. Once the reader gets past these ancient conventions, the message is still vague as to exactly what parcel of land Michael received. Generally, one can surmise that the land borders the Ipswich River and the towns of Salem Village and Wenham. The precise borders might well be a cause for dispute. As matters turned out, indeed the bounds of this land as described in this deed created the problem that could have been predicted using today's conventions.

Deeds worded with this level of exactitude were common. Michael, Sr., would have a problem later in the century as will be described. Michael, Jr., would become involved in this type of problem as a leader in the Topsfield community.

Michael, Jr., appeared to be a universally competent person. Like his father before him, Michael contributed his time and effort to the community. At various times he served as a tithing officer, a hog ringer, a surveyor, a constable, a selectman and the first recorded medical doctor of the community.[5] He raised 13 children and lived an active and productive life until he was 91 years of age.[6] Michael, Jr., had 48 grandchildren.[7] Michael had five wives.[8] As previously stated, it was common for a woman to lead a short life.

This competent man was no stranger to controversy. As one of the region's surveyors, he was directly involved with land disputes with the towns of Wenham and Salem Village. When he was 21 years old, he guarded a woman on trial for witchcraft. The woman he guarded was Sarah Good. She was a quarrelsome woman, somewhat understandably. As matters turned out, she was a challenge as a prisoner.

We should explore these matters more specifically within the context of the total environment that Michael experienced. Topsfield was still a small town in 1691.

The number of houses in Topsfield in the late seventeenth century was about forty. The amount was determined by comparing the number of commoners with the number of church attendees. The result was the estimate of forty.[9] Nearby, Salem Village had a population of 600, with approximately 150 households. Thus, the average household of Salem Village would have been four persons. Using the Salem Village model as an indication of household size in the area, I have set the population of Topsfield at 160 people.

Given the transportation problems of this period in history, the town of Topsfield was quite a distance from Boston, and the threat of Indians was constant. There were little or no printed materials beyond the bible and other religious materials in the home. Word of mouth, sometimes deteriorating to gossip, was the most common form of communication. The local Agawam Indians were not a threat but the Taratine Indians were on the edge of Andover, only two towns to the northwest. Men and sometimes their families from Topsfield and adjacent towns served in Maine, then part of the Massachusetts Bay Colony. The stories of terror created by the nearby unfriendly Indians and the Indians near Freeport, Maine, had its effect on the population.[10] Stories of the dangers of the Maine Indians would add to the level of anxiety of people at home.

Topsfield was still rural, so people were aware of the forest. There was still a bounty on wolves. This environment elicited a plain living and dauntingly hard life. People lived in ordinary houses and worked hard as subsistence farmers. Understandably, their language may have been coarse and their dress flamboyant somewhat in contrast to the dictates of their Puritan religion.[11] The Massachusetts Bay Colony had Puritanism as its state religion.

The local minister played a critical role in community life. This religious person was the moral arbiter of the community. Puritanism as practiced in the Massachusetts Bay Colony was an all-pervasive condition. It was mandatory that all persons be Church attendees. A representative of each family would be a church member, often the woman of the house. Standards were strict, often harsh. The community accepted these standards. A deviation from the norm would have its sociological as well as religious even criminal repercussions.

Sunday sermons were long. The wrath of God would be visited upon the parishioners from the pulpit elevated above the congregation. It was quoted that one Topsfield minister "... could pronounce the word 'damn' with greater emphasis than any man of his time."[12] There were instructional classes during the week as well. The only reading materials in most families were the Bible and some specific religious learning materials.

There were four convictions that contributed to the Puritan religion.

1. Salvation was entirely from God.

2. The Bible provided the indispensable guide to life.

3. The Church should reflect the express teaching of Scripture.

4. Society was one unified whole.[13]

These ideas, particularly that society was one unified whole, had a profound effect on the small, tightly knit communities of Topsfield and adjacent Salem Village. When you consider a frontier society and an omnipresent state religion, it would appear that the community, of necessity and perhaps design, would be cohesive and cooperative. Such was the case in both Topsfield and Salem Village in 1691 when the Salem Witch Trials began in Salem Village. The onset of witchcraft in Salem Village would have its effect on abutting Topsfield—and on Michael Dwinell, Jr.

The incidences of witchcraft in Salem Village have been told and retold in fact and fiction. There are many theories as to why this phenomenon occurred then and at that particular locale. Witchcraft had occurred before in the Colonies and in Europe. Although the experiences in Salem Village and beyond were dramatic, it wasn't a unique phenomenon. The specific origin of the witchcraft outbreak in 1691 appears to be universally accepted. A description of the onset of the 1691 problem in Salem Village appears to be the following.

The local pastor of the Salem Village Puritan Church was Reverend Samuel Parris. His household consisted of himself and his wife, Elizabeth, two of their children, a boy aged 10 and Betty aged 9, a niece named Abigail Williams aged 11, and a Caribbean black slave named Titubia and her husband. This was a rather small household by the norm of the era. It has been stated that Mrs. Parris was not well. Her slave, Titubia, assumed a more significant role in the care of the children than would be the usual case. Titubia was somewhat more permissive than a minister's wife would have been.[14]

The author, Frances Hill, mentions that Reverend Parris' ministerial style was "stark, overbearing, dull, unyielding and unforgiving."[15] This was a typical condition at Puritan Sunday sermons and weekday lectures. It appears that there was a carryover to the Parris household.

Coupled with the stern family presence was the role of girls in family life. Frances Hill describes the plight of these girls as follows: "The lives of young girls were monotonous past bearing and also full of anxiety. They lived, as did everyone, with the constant danger of Indian attacks, serious illness and political upheaval. They also felt the continual need to repress feelings of rebelliousness and rage. The Puritans saw human nature in the starkest possible terms. A person was saintly or sinful, godly or devilish. For a young girl to exhibit anything but docility in the face of her dreary existence was to stir fears that she was thoroughly evil."[16]

Abigail Williams was faced with this plight as she and some other girls escaped to the nearby woods one day in 1691 to play an imaginative game as girls would do. The resultant calamity triggered the witch trials episode that would see large numbers of accusations, prison sentences and even hangings. Central to this imaginative episode was Titubia who confessed to witchcraft. Perhaps she suggested some imaginative activities of her Caribbean heritage. There were two other women involved in this specific incident, Sarah Osborne and Sarah Good.[17]

Michael Dwinell, Jr., sometimes referred to as Michael Dunnell, would have a direct involvement with Sarah Good in one of the most dramatic episodes in this brief but chaotic era in Colonial America. The local constable, Joseph Herrick, Sr., commissioned Michael together with two other men to guard Sarah Good in the Ipswich Jail on the evening of March 1, 1691. The account of that evening is best recounted by the deposition of Joseph Herrick that follows.

"The Deposition of Joseph Herrick senr. Who testifieth and saith that of the first day of March 1691/2: I being then Constable for Salem: there was delivered to me by warrant from the worshipfull Jno. Hathorne and Jonathan Corwin Esqrs, Sarah good for me to cary to their majesties Gaol at Ipswich and that night I sett a gard to watch her at my own house namely Samu'l Braybrook, michaell dunell Jonathan Baker ... and the affore named parsons Informed me in the morning that that night Sarah good was gone for some time from them both bare foot and bare legde: and I was also Informed that: that night Elizabeth Hubburd one of the Afflected parsons Complaned that Sarah Good came and afflected hir: being baare foot and bare ledged and Samuell Sibley that was one that was attending of Eliza Hubburd strock good on the Arme as Elizabeth Hubburd said and Mary Herrick and wife of the abovesaid Joseph Herick testifieth that on the 2th: March 1691/2 in the morning I took notis of Sarah Good in the morning and one of hir Armes was Blooddy from a little below the Elbow to the wrist: and I also took notis of her armes on the night before and then there was no signe of blood on them.

Joseph herrik senr and Mary herrik appeaarid before us the Jury for Inquest: and did on the oath which the had taken owne this their evidence to be the truth the 28: of June 1692.

Sworne in Court

(Reverse) Memento. Sam Sibley to be Served Mich'll Dunwill Jona. Bacar ver. Sa. Good"[18]

Sarah Good had a hard life. She grew up with reasonable wealth and her husband had property. When her husband died, he did not provide for her in his will as she had expected. Sarah became embittered. As a result, she was not well liked in the community. Many historians say she was falsely accused, convicted and hung. There are many accounts of false convictions and hangings during this era.[19]

There are several theories that indicate the cause of the witchcraft outbreaks in Salem Village and the surrounding area. Some writers point to the religion and the tight-knit communities that could be described as a "familiarity breeds contempt" theory. Other theorists point to the many land disputes pitting neighbor against neighbor. A recent theorist ties these theories to the threat of Indian attacks and the more severe and very real Indian attacks in the northern portion of the Massachusetts Bay Colony near what is now Freeport, Maine.[20]

It was an easy matter for the community to have condemned Sarah Good. Her bizarre behavior that involved Michael was perhaps the "last straw" for a community that disliked her. She apparently did not deserve to hang, but her neighbors did not appear to regret her demise.

Other women were arrested, jailed and, in some cases, hung who had considerable community support and were well respected and supported. Two of these people were Rebecca Nurse and Mary Estey.[21] Mary Estey's reaction to her plight was remarkable. An account of her experience as described by George Francis Dow as published in his *History of Topsfield* follows.

"Mary Easty was the most remarkable figure in the history of that terrible time. She seems to have been the only person, man or woman, gentle or simple, who kept her head and knew exactly the thing to do. Women in her station at that time were uneducated. Most of them could not write their names. Yet, we find her in the midst of this great excitement, while in prison and on trial for her life, presenting a petition to the Judges which, as a legal document, equals anything written by the leading lawyers of the day. It seems reasonable to conclude that to this document she owed her release." Dow goes on to directly quote the document itself as follows.

"The humble Request of Mary Esty and Sarah Cloys to the Honoured Court.

Humbly shewth, that wheras we two Sisters Mary Esty and Sarah Cloys stand now before the Honoured court charged with the suspition of Witchcraft, our hmble request is first that seeing we are neither able to plead our owne cause, nor is councell alowed to those in our condicion, that you whyo are our Judges, wuld please to be of councell to us, to direct us wher in; we may stand in neede, Secondly, that whereas we are not conscious to ourselves of any guilt in the least degree of that crime, wherof we are now accused In the presence of ye Living God we speake it, before whose awfull Tribunall we know we shall ere Long appeare) nor of any other scandalouse evill, or miscaryage inconsistant with Christianity, Those who have had ye Longest and best knowledge of vs, being persons of good report, may be suffered to Testifie upon oath what they know concerning each of vs. viz Mr. Capen, the pastour and those of ye Towne and Church of Topsfield, who are ready to say something which we hope may be looked upon, as very considerable in this matter: with the seven children of one of us, viz Mary Esty, and it may be produced of like nature in reference to the wife of Peter Cloys, her sister, Thirdly, that the Testimony of witches, or such, as are afflicted, as is supposed, by witches may not be improved to condemn us, without other Legal evidence concurring, we hope the honoured Court and Jury will be soe tender of the lives of such as we are who have for many yeares Lived vnder the vnblemished reputation of Christianity as not to condemne them without a fare and equall hearing of what may be sayd for us, as well as against us, And your poore supplyants shall be bound always to pray &c." (Essex Co. Court Records)

In a second plea to the court, Mary Esty said, in part.

". I Petition to your honours not for my own life for I know I myst die and my appointed time is sett but the Lord he knowes it is that if it be possible no more Innocent blood may be shed which undoubtedly cannot be Avoydd In the way and course you goe in ... I beg you honers not to deny this my humble petition from a poor dying Innocent person and I Question not but the Lord will giue a blesing to your endeuers." (Essex Co. Court Records.) For these two efforts, she is called "Mary Easty, the self forgetful." She was executed September 22, 1692 on Gallows hill in Salem.[22]

There are heroes and heroines in many dire situations. Mary Estey was such a heroine. She was a contemporary of Michael Dwinell, Jr., and a fellow resident of Topsfield. The Estey and the Towne families were influential in Topsfield. Mary Estey's maiden name was Mary Towne. She was aware of her rights as an English subject. Many of the rights she alluded to were from the Magna Carta. Some were from recent negotiations between the Massachusetts Bay Colony and England. Ultimately, Mary Estey was hung for witchcraft despite her heroic plea.

As the aftermath of the witchcraft trials faded, Michael, as well as his father, would be involved in the border disputes that triggered much of the rancor and the resultant outbreak of accusations. As the witchcraft episodes faded in Salem Village, they would emerge in other communities. In fact, they soon broke out in Topsfield.

The land disputes are mentioned by most of the most famous authors who have researched the Salem Witch Trials. One source co authored by Mrs. Abbie Peterson Towne and Miss Marietta Clark point out that the witch accusations made against Topsfield people were almost exclusively the result of land disputes. The authors claim that the dispute began as a result of a clerical error made by the General Court in 1639. Topsfield was created as a result of land contributions of several towns. Once again, the language was ambiguous. The Putnam family of

Salem Village had a great deal to do with the resultant disputes. In 1680 a committee was formed in Topsfield to investigate the issue. Several more committees would be formed over the years and Michael Dwinell, Sr. and Jr. would be involved.[23]

The expression witchcraft and "witch hunt" entered our vocabulary following this era. There would be future witch-hunts. Heroes and heroines would emerge, but as occurred in Salem Village in 1691 and 1692, lives would be damaged, ruined or even lost. There was much that was learned from the Salem Witch Trials. It is a memorial to the weakness of man that we repeat the witchcraft syndrome periodically through history.

A case in point was the McCarthy Hearings of the early 1950s. Senator Joseph McCarthy of Wisconsin set out to rid our government of communists and communist influence. In the process he ruined lives and postponed careers of people who were falsely accused.

People know as the result of the Salem and McCarthy experiences that the mere accusation does not make a person guilty. Peer pressure can be a powerful force. This phenomenon along with gossip and the use of inconclusive evidence cleverly manipulated can ruin lives and frighten entire communities and even nations. For some reason, humanity fails to learn from these experiences.

The guarding of Sarah Good was the first community responsibility of Michael Dwinell, Jr.[24]; Michael was 21 years of age. Michael soon became a surveyor, thus becoming part of the land disputes that continued between neighbors and between towns.

The witchcraft episodes abated after 1692 but the social climate brought on by the religion, political conditions, warfare, Indian threats, medical problems and land disputes would remain. Dr. Michael Dwinell, Jr., played an important role in Topsfield as the eighteenth century arrived.

After Michael's guard experience, he next served the town as a surveyor of highways. At the same time he would follow in his father's footsteps as one of the town's hog ringers. As the years went by, he would have more surveying responsibility as the town surveyor.[25]

Topsfield records indicate that he was asked to "perambulate the bounds", particularly, the boundaries of Topsfield and Wenham as well as Salem Village.

The casual nature of the original deeds caused the land disputes to continue. Michael assumed these surveying duties in 1730 and again in 1736. The town found it necessary to defend his father, Michael, Sr., against a boundary dispute with Salem Village in 1694. This dispute was near the land that Michael, Jr., had acquired.[26]

Michael was chosen as a constable in 1706 and again in 1720 and 1733. He served as a selectman in 1716 and 1724 and served on juries in 1718, 1723 and 1726. However, Michael is best known as the first recorded medical doctor of Topsfield. Topsfield had had medical services before from the doctors in Salem Town.[27] As the town grew it was necessary for Topsfield to have its own doctor, and Michael was asked to assume this role. We should explore what it was like to be an eighteenth century town doctor.

The assumption of the role of doctor in a small colonial town in America was indeed a challenge. Like many of his counterparts in other towns, there appears to be no evidence that Michael had any formal medical training.

Even in the cities of Boston or Salem, there were limited medical facilities on a par with London or other European centers of power, wealth and culture. Often, in the colonies, the role of doctor fell to competent men such as ministers or community leaders.

Michael appears to have been a competent man. Evidently the community appreciated his leadership qualities. His role as town surveyor suggests a scientific point of view and a pragmatic objectivity.

To appreciate Michael's role as a small town doctor, we should look at the profession of medicine as it had evolved up to the time of Michael's assumption of this task. Then, we should look at the practice of medicine by the laymen of small town Colonial America.

The Greek civilization has been credited with an impressive competence in medicine. As early as the fifth century, B.C., Greek thinkers were preoccupied with disease and its cure. Hippocrates organized and developed a body of medical thought, the Corpus Hippocratium, in about 400–450 BC[28] Many of the medical principles of Hippocrates and other ancient medical thinkers that contributed to his work are in use today.

Scientific progress has continued from 500, BC, to the current day. Michael Dwinell assumed the role of the town doctor of Topsfield in the early eighteenth century. Recent scientific findings of the era would help the sophisticated medical practitioner.

But, how much of this body of recent scientific, medically related knowledge did Michael possess? Also, how much of this forward thinking knowledge was available to him in Boston or Salem? Nevertheless, Michael and "doctors" like him tried to help people.

A case in point is the dilemma of Dr. Griggs of Salem Village in 1691. Frances Hill points out to us that he was asked by Samuel Parris to examine his children when his daughters had the dramatic reactions in early 1691. Dr. Griggs had no medical answer to the symptoms, so he concluded that the children were under a spell, perhaps demonic, hence, the onset of the witchcraft scare. Author Hill, several centuries later, has a plausible argument that the children may have been suffering from encephalitis. It would be reasonable to assume that the good Dr. Griggs would have no specific knowledge of this disease, as Ms. Hill points out.

At the least, Michael would use traditional remedies such as lotions, syrups and salves for insect bites and for colds, aches and pains, indigestion and minor injuries and diseases. Some herbs were used. He would have bandaged injuries and cared for the bed ridden. Perhaps a mid-wife was available to help him with the birth of children.

There are many other "home" remedies that were used by town doctors in their efforts to help their patients. A writer describing the medical experience in Topsfield says by contrast "In England the touch of the royal monarch was considered to cure king's evil and scrofula, it is not strange, therefore, that some lingering faith in the absurd customs should crop out in New England."[29] Scrofula is the swelling of the glands often associated with tuberculosis. There were many somewhat quaint remedies that the country doctor had at his disposal. Even in Europe, medicine was far different than it is today. A well-intentioned man in a rural community of an English colony would indeed have a challenge.

Dr. Dwinell entrusted his practice to Amos Dwinell, his nephew, as the practice of medicine in Topsfield continued.[30] England found that the economic return from the colonies was less than expected. As a result, the mother country did not feel compelled to provide medical expertise or facilities to the colonies. Doctors such as Michael only had each other and whatever expertise may have been available in larger communities such as Salem Town and Boston.

Michael Dwinell, Jr., deserves credit for having established the role of the town doctor of Topsfield. His role must have been frustrating at times. He must have known that a greater body of knowledge existed elsewhere. Even today with instantaneous communication and more available, speedy and safe transportation, some country doctors feel isolated. The role of country doctor of eighteenth century Topsfield was indeed a challenge.

A description of the basic economic climate of the Massachusetts Bay Colony would reveal the nature of the life of the colonist. There was a clear distinction between the cities of Boston and Salem and life in the small towns such as Topsfield.

The colonists in the hinterland communities were subsistence farmers. The colonists in the larger communities such as Salem Town and Boston were the owners of commercial businesses. While the farmers were left to themselves, the business people could trade with the colonists and with England. Both groups of people would have difficulties with this economic proposition.

The people of the Massachusetts Bay Colony were living under the economic system of mercantilism as the seventeenth century came to a close. Most observers indicate that mercantilism practices began in Europe in about 1550.[31] Mercantilism is an outgrowth from feudalism as nation states looked outward to competition from other countries.

To the ordinary English peasant, the transition from feudalism to mercantilism had little effect on their lives. Except for the distance from the mother country, the colonists in America had many of the same problems as the English peasant. The colonists, though, had the advantage of apparent land ownership and a degree of freedom. We should look at feudalism, first. Then, we should see how the colonist needed to adapt to English mercantilist practices.

English feudal rule began with William I, or as he is better known, William the Conqueror.[32] As the invading French Duke of Normandy, he needed to rule by force and rigid political and economic domination. After his successful invasion of England in 1066, he set up a system of government based on a direct and indirect loyalty to him as the king. He needed this loyalty, since he was also the Duke of Normandy who had to protect his interests in France.

William's immediate subordinates were those noblemen who were loyal to him as he defeated the English in the Battle of Hastings.[33] As he then eventually controlled all of England, he realized that he could not control this total domain himself.

Lands of the king were entrusted to his tenants in chief. These persons were the barons, earls and dukes who had sworn allegiance to the King. It is important to note that these royal figures did not actually own the land, but they were entrusted with the land to protect the interests of the king.[34]

The barons would then divide the responsibility for land management to the knights who had also fought for the king. These knights would act as the sub tenants of the land to protect the manorial system. The land of the king was divided into manors. A manor would be the size of a county as is known today in England.[35]

William I and future kings would supervise this enterprise through a device known as the Doomsday Book.[36] This book would account for all of the holdings of each sub division of the king's realm.

The peasant was under the direct control of the reeve, the local manager. In many respects the peasant was comparable to a tenant farmer of today. The peasant of the era of William I and II had little or no freedom in this severely rigid line organization previously described.

This feudal system evolved over the next 500 years as various laws were enacted to provide more rights to those who lived on English land. The royal control of this land diminished over this period.[37] Other countries of Europe had comparable systems. In a feudal system, the peasant paid taxes to the king and tithes to the Church in money or in kind. The peasant was also tied to the farming year. It was expected that production would proceed as planned throughout each year.

The peasant of England, Europe and throughout the known world had a bleak outlook. The philosopher, Thomas Hobbes, was to describe their life as "solitary, poor, nasty, brutish and short."[38]

The colonists in America had been granted land. They were free to farm this land for subsistence and for local commerce. In reality, this land was granted to the colonists to be under the control of the king. The control was rather loosely administered. It might be said that the king retained de jure control but the colonist had de facto control.

Dr. Michael Dwinell would also serve as a surveyor in this confusing environment. It has been mentioned that the preciseness of deeds was lacking. The nature of ownership was also in question. Mercantilist control was evident.

In return, the mother country expected that these colonists would purchase imports from England, and it was not expected that the colonists would trade with countries other than England. Beyond the sustained feudal environment of England and the colonists controlled lives in America, a competitive world existed. Thus, a transition was occurring from the internal trappings of feudalism to the external trappings of mercantilism. As mercantilism is explored, the reader will see how this economic force of commercial capitalism or mercantilism led to competition, controversy, and even war.

The transition from feudalism to mercantilism occurred gradually. The economic system of mercantilism relates to the behavior of kings rather than the peasants and serfs constituting the majority of the people. The king vied for control against the lesser lords of his realm as well as the kings of other nations. This need for relative control and power required a particular style of economic behavior.

The economic actions of the kingdom were designed to create power and wealth within one's own kingdom while attempting to lessen power within the realm of one's competitive nation state. England acted in such a manner so as to strengthen England while weakening France, Spain, Holland, and/or Portugal.

The colonies of England existed only to strengthen the well being of the mother country. Meanwhile, England's' competitors were acting in a similar fashion. The mother country would decide what commercial activities would take place in its colonies. The expeditions to Maine at the time of the Witch Trials were created to obtain huge poles for ship masts acquired from the Great American Forest. This action would enrich the mother country by creating a stronger merchant fleet and military navy. By implication this economic action would relatively weaken England's competitors.

England would decide what goods were to be imported to America from England by the colonists. Exports from the colonies were controlled by England. In short, England was to do everything possible to maintain a favorable balance of trade relative to its competitive nations. The rural colonists lived at subsistence and traded amongst themselves. England would not tolerate any activity beyond this description.

The original settlers of the colonies had experienced a strict feudal existence. The American experience produced relative freedom and the advantage of land ownership. As future colonists attempted to expand this freedom, England would react.

Dr. Michael Dwinell witnessed this escalating turmoil and perhaps predicted the impending unrest. He led a long and fruitful life living until he was 91 years old. He saw the onset of the Colonial Wars and saw his sons go off to war. He became his community's first doctor and performed many other roles in the community. The generations to follow would benefit from the examples he set.

The next two generations would experience the revolutionary activity that would be a precursor of the Revolutionary War, the war itself and the adjustment to a new life in the climate of an emerging country.

He left a legacy of community leadership. The model he established for his family would be beneficial to them as they faced the uncertainty of revolution and war.

We should turn first to the life of Benjamin who fought in both the Colonial Wars and the Revolutionary War. Then his son, Thomas, who would also fight in the Revolutionary War. As they lived their lives in Topsfield and then Boxford and Keene, they would live their lives as citizen soldiers.

3

Benjamn The Soldier

"What's all this fuss about a few acres of snow?"

—Voltaire

"We are all animated with the spirit of an industry which is unfettered and unrestrained, because each person works for himself."

—de Crevecoeur

Benjamin was the fifth son of Michael Dwinell, Jr. His mother was Elizabeth Fisk Dwinell. She was Michael Dwinell's second wife. Benjamin was born on November 10, 1726, in Topsfield, Massachusetts. He is my great, great, great, great grandfather.

Benjamin was married to Mary Estey on February 25, 1751.[1] Mary Estey is the granddaughter of the Mary Easty who was involved in the witchcraft crisis in Salem Village, Topsfield and elsewhere in the 1691–92 eras.[2]

Benjamin and Mary Dwinell would live with Dr. Michael Dwinell until Michael's death in 1761. Dr. Dwinell's will states that Benjamin would inherit the "house and barn, and my land and meadow in Topsfield."[3] The will distributed money to other members of the family and did not mention the distribution of any other lands, even though Benjamin was the fifth son of Michael, Jr.

It was common practice in the eighteenth century for families to provide land to one member of the family upon the death of the father. Usually, land was distributed during the life of the father. This practice was continued to avoid the division of land into such small parcels that the use of the land for farming would be unproductive. The search of deeds of the era would reveal that this distribution took place in the case of the Dwinell family and other families.

Benjamin became a farmer on the land willed to him by his father.[4] This land was in the Wenham Road and Salem Road area of Topsfield. Salem Road is one of the main roads going east out of Topsfield. As mentioned in Chapters One and Two, the land on this road was the subject of some controversy in the mid-1690s when Benjamin's grandfather, Michael Dwinell, Sr., owned parcels of land on both sides of Salem Road which bordered Salem Village. Evidently, they would live in quiet enjoyment as Benjamin and Mary would have ten children.[5] Four of these children would be born in Topsfield.

As Benjamin worked as a farmer in Topsfield, preparations for conflict were taking place. He would be involved in military training in 1745 with his brothers Jacob and Michael, 2nd.[6] It is interesting to note that Dr. Michael's son, Michael, 2nd, is not Michael, 3rd. There were many variations of the first name of Dr. Michael Dwinell's father. One variation often used was Mikal.

As an outgrowth of this local military training, Benjamin was part of a force that went to Cape Britten, probably Cape Breton, in 1745 to successfully capture the fort at Louisbourg.[7] Benjamin was 19. As we shall see, this action marked the beginning of a rather active military career for Benjamin Dwinell. He was a member of the Topsfield militia at this point in his life.[8]

The battle to secure Fort Louisbourg for the English was an important battle in King George's War in July, 1745. Fort Louisbourg was referred to as the "Gibralter of the New World." The victory enhanced the reputation of colonial forces in Massachusetts and caused the English to provide the Massachusetts colony with almost 184,000 English pounds. This added hard currency would allow the Colony to establish a sounder currency for merchant transactions.[9] The battle for Fort Louisbourg was also unique in that the English forces, mostly Massachusetts Bay militia, attacked the fort from inland rather than by sea. This condition was instrumental in its success.

A sense of the Battle of Louisbourg is captured in a quote from Richard M. Ketchum in his book entitled *The Battle for Bunker Hill* as he talks about the colonel responsible for the fortifications at the Battle of Bunker Hill when he states "he may have been reminded of that June day thirty years ago, when the young Lieutenant Colonel Gridley's gunners, throwing shell after shell into the supposedly impregnable fortress of Louisbourg, had forced the Frenchmen to run and dive into the sea to escape the fiery hail of death."[10]

The British had organized the men of each town into a militia. Ostensibly to defend the town against Indian raids, this militia also served as a military force against the French in the outlying districts of America. There is a marked resemblance between the militia of Colonial America and the National Guard of the several states of our country today. The National Guard serves each state as its militia but is available as a fighting unit in the event of national military action.

The aftermath of the Fort Louisbourg victory would have its political overtones that would haunt the English decades later. The English gave the fort back to the French in diplomatic negotiations soon after the battle. This action threatened the well being of the colonies fishing industry and left a bitter pill in the mouths of the colonists.

Benjamin lived in this period of unrest. He would see other Topsfield men go off to fight in far away places against the French. They considered themselves to be English and were happy to fight for their country. This war activity would soon hit home.

Benjamin would realize that his brother, Michael, had died in Topsfield as a result of action in Quebec in 1754. Michael had been captured in the Quebec area. It had been reported that he was safe, but soon thereafter, he had died when he returned home to Topsfield. Michael was the second oldest son of Dr. Michael Dwinell.

It would have been reasonable to suspect that Michael had become ill while in captivity. Becoming ill while in the military was a life-threatening situation. Hospitals were hardly able to care for the soldier. Doctors were assigned to specific units and were not necessarily available to give care to hospitalized patients. Commanders did not want soldiers returned to their units prematurely. The commanders felt that these soldiers would malinger and/or desert. Often soldiers were released to their own devices to get home on their own. This choice would be extremely dangerous given the existence of hostile Indians.

There is no clear indication as to where Michael Dwinell served on the Eastern Frontier near Quebec or how he became ill. The explanation of illness is presented here to describe the health conditions facing the Colonial soldier.

It is recorded that Benjamin enlisted in the Company of Captain Israel Davis on March 16, 1756.[11] It was customary for soldiers to enlist in the spring of the year[12] and to serve for relatively short periods of time. To a large extent these men were farmers, including Benjamin. Benjamin became a corporal on November 29, 1756, as he served at Fort William Henry at Lake George, New York. Later records of Captain Davis show that Benjamin served as a corporal from March 16 until November 17, 1756, and as a sergeant from November 20, 1756, until February 1, 1757.[13] The apparent conflict in dates may be due to the formal orders regarding his promotion to sergeant being delayed. Another record has Benjamin mustering out of military service as a sergeant on January 31, 1757.[14] It would appear reasonable to state that Benjamin served as a sergeant from the beginning of December, 1756, to the end of January, 1757. There is no reliable record available to indicate Benjamin's military service to the English after February, 1757. Perhaps he did muster in again. There are many spellings of the name Dwinell in the Massachusetts Archives for the Colonial Wars. Each one of these references would need to be pursued with considerable care to be certain of Benjamin's future military involvement. Captain Israel Davis was present at the Fort William Henry Massacre in August, 1757. Perhaps Benjamin served once again as one of Captain Davis' sergeants.

Benjamin had served under Captain Davis on the Crown Point expedition and with Captain Davis and Colonel Jonathan Bagley at Fort William Henry. He had already seen a good deal of combat and the results of combat.[15]

The fall of 1756 was a critical time in the Seven Years' War. The French had assembled a sizable force of Indians at Fort Carrillon (the French name for Fort Ticonderoga) to the north. The soldiers at Fort William Henry realized that the French commanders were having difficulty controlling these Indians whom they had assembled. The French had control of a vast area of geography constituting the inland areas of what is now southern Canada and northern United States to the Mississippi River. There were many Indian tribes in this wide expanse. Each tribe had a different culture and different motivation. The promises of the French to the Indians left the Indians impatient and anxious for the fulfillment of their mission.

The Indians began to receive a reputation they did not deserve at this point in history. The French had entered their land and interacted with them to help the French war effort against the British. The British had colonized the lands of the Indians causing them to move farther westward as the decades went by. The Indians were caught between these great powers and reacted. Life for a soldier alone or with a small group of men was dangerous once they left the fort and were traveling in the Great American Forest, the domain of the Indian.

When you consider Benjamin's situation on February 1, 1757, you need to understand that he had to get home. As mustering out processes worked, the company commanders would have recruited from a specific geographic area. In the case of Captain Israel Davis, it was in the Boxford, Topsfield and Wenham areas and other nearby communities. These men would then be under his command. Upon mustering out, this company of men would travel toward home together. Fort William Henry is about 200 miles from the Topsfield area. Men traveled at about 30 miles a day. It would take a week or more for these men to get home. Given the presence of the Indians, it would be a dangerous trip. This trip took place in the dead of winter.

You can acquire an insight to the problems facing colonists on their return home as you read James Fenimore Cooper's *The Last of the Mohicans*.[16] This is a novel about the aftermath of the Fort William Henry Massacre. At one point in the novel, the heroes of the story were attempting to avoid the Indians who were in the Lake George area.

In the novel, *The Last of the Mohicans*, the soldiers are traveling across the top of hills looking down on the Indians on the shore of Lake George. As Benjamin started home, he would have to avoid well-traveled areas as well and be alert to possible Indians in the area. He would also have to be ready to avoid a confrontation. Benjamin was a sergeant at this point. It is conceivable that he was in charge of the men returning home while Captain Davis remained at Fort William Henry.

As the provincial soldiers of early 1757 marched home across New York and then New England, they were confronted by the possibility of Indian attack. The Indians were a frightening force with whom to contend. Perhaps urged on by the French, perhaps as a reaction to the French or perhaps as a result of mal treatment by the English, it was rumored that these Indians indulged in horrifying practices. The rigors of winter were not Benjamin's only problem.

Ian Steele in his book, *Betrayals* Fort William Henry and the "Massacre", provided two rather grisly quotes from a French source. The first observation stated that the Indians "have eaten an English officer whose pallor and plumpness tempted them. Such cruelties are frequent enough among the Indians of LaBelle Riviere. Our domesticated Indians, softened by the glimmerings of Christianity which they have received, are no longer cruel in cold blood, but one cannot say, however, that their character is changed." Another quote stated "demanding broth which is to say blood, drawn 500 leagues by the smell of fresh human flesh and the opportunity to teach their youths how to cut up a person destined for the cook pot. These are the comrades who are our shadows day and night. I shudder at the ghastly spectacles which they are preparing for us."[17]

These observations were from a French source. As the war progressed, it would become difficult to determine who would find the Indians a more dangerous threat, the French, the English or the Provincial soldiers from the colonies.

The Indians were victims of the white man's presence and manipulation. After 15,000 years of independent living, these various peoples were placed in a frightening situation, and they reacted. The condescending superior attitudes of both the French and the English did not help matters.

There were various routes that Benjamin and his comrades could have taken. They could have traveled south to Fort Edward near Albany, New York, and then east toward the Massachusetts Bay Colony. Fort Massachusetts was near the present Adams, Massachusetts, near the New York border. After Fort Massachusetts there would be a long trek across mountains and through a dense forest toward Deerfield, Massachusetts.

The danger of Indians would have subsided as the group approached the Connecticut River, perhaps. Another route would have been directly across southern Vermont along what is now called the Molly Stark Trail. This journey would have taken them toward Fort Dummer near the present Brattleboro, Vermont. The most direct route would have been to travel into the present state of Vermont, called at the time, the New Hampshire Grants. This route would have taken the men through the mountains to the Fort at Number Four in Charleston, New Hampshire. One should remember that these forts and other lesser forts were available to protect nearby residents from Indian raids and act as military staging areas. Although the journey would become less dangerous as the men headed east, they had to be alert.

In 1756 "the war on the settlers (at the Fort at Number Four) continued. It was the intent of the French and Indians to drive the settlers out of the Upper Valley (of the Connecticut River) back to Deerfield (MA). Many petitions were sent for aid, supplies and more soldiers during this turbulent time. On June 18, 1756, Lt. Moses Willard, Mrs. Johnson's father, went to extinguish a fire in his fence set by the Indians, and lost his life. His son was wounded in the hip by a spear, but was able to escape and reach the safety of the fort.... early spring (1757) saw an outbreak of smallpox."[18] Even at a fort set up to control the Indians and to accommodate the movement of troops to the location of battle, dangers lurked. The men had to move from fort to fort. They were not necessarily guaranteed safety when they reached each fort.

Sanitary conditions at these smaller forts and even the larger forts in New York—Fort Edward and Fort William Henry—were horrible. There was almost as much danger from the living conditions created at the forts as there was from the enemy.[19] Yet, they traveled home. There was a family waiting—in Benjamin's case, his wife and four children. Also, there was a farm to tend. In Benjamin's case, he would be home by mid February if all went well. Then, he could prepare his farm for growth. Perhaps he would be recalled. Perhaps he faced further military service with mixed emotions.

Despite the dangers, there was an advantage to military service. The money earned might buy more land or the provisions necessary for the farm business. Soldiers were not paid until the end of their term of service. This money could serve them well in a society where hard currency was at a premium.[20]

It was a common practice for units to muster out in the fall. This mid-winter mustering appeared to be atypical. Typically, troops mustered back in as the spring arrived. Captain Israel Davis did remain on duty at Fort William Henry. My research has not revealed a mustering-in process that would have Benjamin once again part of the Massachusetts regiment at Fort William Henry. The Massachusetts 35th Regiment was one of the regiments attacked by Indians at the Fort William Henry Massacre. Topsfield men answered the alarm to march toward Fort William Henry in early-August, 1757, as the impending battle loomed.[21]

The English had consolidated operations early in 1757.[22] Prior to this consolidation, the colonists were organized as provincial troops under the command of a colonel of a regiment composed of other provincial soldiers. These provincial regiments were separate from the English Regulars who were under the command of an English Regular Army Colonel. The consolidation would have a different effect upon the life of the colonists.

The English commanders were accustomed to the British soldiers. The enlisted soldiers of the English military were the dregs of a class-conscious society. In Fred Anderson's *A Peoples Army*, he states "the rank and file of the regular army was composed of permanently marginal members of British society. Convicts, vagabonds, sundry social misfits, and natives of the impoverished back-country of Scotland and Ireland traditionally constituted a great portion of the king's troops. As the eighteenth century wore on these were increasingly joined by people cast adrift by enclosure and industrialization ... respectable folk whose positions in society had been eroded in an era of rapid economic change."[23] Anderson points out further that the Massachusetts soldiers were "by no means colonial proletarians."[24]

The colonial, or provincial, soldier had a farm to manage or an artisan's business to conduct. He was only available for a limited period of time. Also, the class-conscious English officer would have no difficulty ordering the subservient British lower class to do his bidding. The American colonist was another consideration, as the British would discover. The colonist had lived in relative freedom. They still had an allegiance to the mother country, England, but they were left to fend for themselves. This freedom was particularly characteristic of the small town artisan, laborer or farmer. It was not customary for anyone to be telling these people what to do

Although independent of spirit, the typical colonist was a member of the Congregational religion, the successor to Puritanism. These people believed in community. Their allegiance was to the community, their natural environment, not necessarily the English authority.[25] Although the residents of Massachusetts appeared to show deference to the elite class, they did not conform to the existence of royalty as did their counterparts in England. Many of the vestiges of feudalism were still present in England. The Massachusetts Bay Colony was essentially an egalitarian society.

In America, these Provincial soldiers owned their own land or were workers in a community. The Massachusetts Bay colonist was not as subservient to the upper class British officer as the regular army British soldier would have been.

It was critical to the operation of a finely balanced economy for the potential colonial soldiers to be available in the towns in which they lived. The economy was a unique form of social balance between laborer, artisan and farmer. There was little or no currency available in the agrarian portion of the Massachusetts Bay economy. Accounts would be kept among the town's families regarding the activity and goods produced in the local economy.

A farmer would produce goods for local consumption. An artisan would produce the results of his labor and talent. The laborer would produce the result of his toil. Each of these activities had a different "price" and these respective costs were tabulated with considerable care.[26] The young man was in a critical position. Typically, the young man was as valuable as the work he could provide. He did not yet own land.

Although there was a lack of currency in the agricultural sector of the colonial economy, there was currency in the mercantile sector. The Colony had created a specie, or form of money, fashioned after the English Pound Sterling. The Colonial specie did not have the same intrinsic value as the English Pound Sterling, but it served as a vehicle for commercial transactions. Ultimately, the exchange rate set between the English Pound Sterling and the Colonial Pound of the Massachusetts Bay Colony was to be 1:00 to 1:33. It would take 1.33 Colonial Pounds to equal one English Pound Sterling, because the English Pound Sterling was backed by Sterling Silver.[27]

It is customary throughout history for farmers to be money poor and land rich. It is necessary for the farmer to use available funds and to borrow in order to obtain resources to grow the product and then to wait for the harvest. This colonial experience in Massachusetts was an exaggerated case of this virtually universal economic condition.

This exaggerated situation was a product of monetary mercantilism. Mercantilism attempts to maintain a favorable balance of trade for the mother country in order to have wealth accrue to the home country. In addition to this trade condition, England did not want the Pound Sterling to be leaving England, hence the shortage of hard currency and even specie in the hinterlands of the colony.

A young man without an artisan's skill and without land was at some disadvantage. His value to the community and to his family was the strength of his back. How much manual labor could he accomplish in a day was the economic measure of his worth. The artisan had a clear advantage.[28]

Typically, young and old men would not possess land. The land of a family would be carefully distributed to the men of the family ready to pursue a career in farming. In the case of Benjamin, the farmland remaining in his father, Michael's, hands when he died was willed to Benjamin in 1762. Either Benjamin was tending the farm for his father or he was a day laborer—perhaps both or perhaps an artisan. Dr. Michael Dwinell appears to have planned the use of the disposition of his land intelligently so that his family was apportioned land as Michael's life progressed, yet the elderly man was not left land-impoverished as old age loomed.

There was one other variation to this description of land tenure. Sometimes land was left to a daughter. The idea of this arrangement was that her husband would run the farm. The Estey family was an important Topsfield family.

Nevertheless, you can see the advantage of military service. Benjamin was able to earn hard currency as a corporal and a sergeant. The mustering out orders of January 31, 1757, indicates that he earned one pound, two shillings.[29] Obviously, this amount is not a king's ransom. It is quite a bit of money, though, when you consider that the greatest amount of money that his father left in his will to any one person was five shillings. A shilling is a fraction of a pound.

As the Seven Years' War continued, the English would prevail. Simultaneous to this effort on the American continent, the English were also waging war in Europe. England would wage war with France until the late 1770s. Even though England would emerge victorious, it would be expensive for the mother country. The Colonies would bear a good deal of the burden.

As the Seven Years' War continued, the colonial soldiers would react. These provincial soldiers were not treated with same deference from British commanders as they had been accustomed to receiving from Colonial officers. The British, for example, would stretch the term of service of the provincial forces beyond the terms of enlistment. There were strikes and mutinies and reprisals.[30]

Yet, Anderson maintains that the returning soldier anticipated life to be improved in a prosperous colonial society now that war was over in America.[31] Surprisingly, the returning Provincial soldier did not seem to bear a grudge against the English. These soldiers were still ready to contribute to the still English society as the mid-1760s arrived.

Life would continue for Benjamin and his fellow colonists. Mary and Benjamin would have six more children between 1759 and 1772. These children would enter a different world. War was imminent and the aftermath to war would provide freedom but hardship as well.

The society was no longer the simple subsistence-farming existence that was experienced in the seventeenth century. There was an increased merchant activity in the principal cities. Despite a lack of hard currency, there was a more sophisticated life in the hinterlands, and the inhabitants of these outer communities had a better understanding of what was happening in Europe. There was a demonstration effect that had its reaction on these people. People in the hinterlands could see the effect of merchant activity on the well-to-do Tories of the cities. By inference, they could see what life in England would be like.

Gradually, there was an emergence from mercantilism to capitalism across Europe but principally in England. The textile industry would be the forerunner of other examples of capital concentration. Mercantilism still existed for the colonist, since, legally, they could only trade with England. The merchant class of the colonies had other ideas as the century progressed.

The decade of the 1760s would see dramatic events that would lead ultimately to revolution. The towns of Topsfield and Boxford would be involved as would every Massachusetts Bay Colony town and the communities of the other colonies under control of the British. Life would continue for the colonist, but life would not be the same as it was. There was a degree of freedom in the colonies including the Massachusetts Bay Colony. Massachusetts, though, was still a British Colony, so there was a class structure present, although not as pronounced as in England.

There was a seeming paradox regarding the socially elite and the democracy in the small towns. The rich and powerful had a social status and the townspeople had their democratic expression. The townspeople would elect the socially elite to positions of importance and defer to their judgment.[32] Yet, these townspeople had their opinions and were willing to express them. The elite class was educated; the rest of the townspeople for the most part were not. They were uneducated, but as matters turned out they were not fools.

Liquor was in abundance in the colonies, and the local tavern served as a meeting place for the community.[33] Much was resolved at these meetings. The informal organization was a powerful force. Thus, the status quo was the existence of a wealthy merchant upper class and the common man living an agrarian existence. The merchant class lived in the larger cities for the most part. There was a somewhat smaller educated upper class in many small communities as well. The day to day and year to year activities accommodated this sociology—until 1765. At this point in history, the British imposed the Stamp Act on the colonies. Life in the Massachusetts Bay Colony would change.

The Stamp Act placed a tax on any transaction requiring the creation of a piece of paper. Today, there are stamps affixed to a deed as a cost of recording this deed. Buyers and sellers of property accept this reasonable tax. The conveyance of property stamps was only one example of the stamps necessary under the stamp act. Every written transaction required a stamp, hence a tax.

The Stamp Act was created to pay for the continued conflict that England had with France. The colonists did not see why this tax was necessary, since the French had been driven from the continent. The embattled farmer living in an essentially barter economy had little or no patience with the imposition of a tax on his limited store of money.[34] However, more than the economic consequences, the small town farmer resented the imposition of authority. The wealthy, large city merchants had some difficulty controlling the reaction of the small town people. Even though the incidence of the Stamp tax and other British measures had a greater total monetary effect on the merchants, the farmers reacted more militantly. Ray Raphael in his book *The First American Revolution,* points out that the impetus for revolution was to a large degree small-town oriented. The farmer liked his freedom and did not want a government 3,000 miles away to dictate his well being.

The deed stamps we know of today is a cost we are used to paying for the conveyance of property. However, the stamps on a deed are only one example. Virtually every business transaction required a stamp at a price to be paid to England. The colonists reacted. There were angry crowds and stamp distributors were hung in effigy. The resultant behavior stopped the distribution of stamps. Without stamps, business could not be transacted. Real property could not be conveyed. As a result, the courts needed to close. The cry of "Taxation without representation" had been effective.[35]

The colonists still looked upon themselves as British subjects with all of the rights of an English citizen. These colonists felt that their rights had been ignored. They reacted. The Stamp Act was repealed in 1766. Over the next decade the colonists would continue to react to other British measures.

In 1692, many decades prior, Mary Estey had mentioned the freedoms that had been denied to her at her Witch Trial. These Freedoms came from the Magna Carta, The Body of Liberties of the Massachusetts Bay Colony and recently instituted English law. She felt that she was a British subject and should be accorded these rights. The 1766 colonists felt the same way.[36]

In this atmosphere, Benjamin and his wife, Mary, would tend their farm in Topsfield recently inherited from Benjamin's father, Dr. Michael Dwinell. At first, this political activity would not have an effect on the average farmer. As the decade went by, the average farmer in the small towns of the Massachusetts Bay Colony would feel the effects of this turmoil.

In addition to the turmoil created by the Stamp Act and other British measures, there was the imposition of the effects of a recession in Europe, England and eventually America. Poverty became an issue in America and this condition exacerbated the turmoil created by English restrictions.

The militia still existed and Benjamin remained a member of the militia both in Topsfield and when he and Mary and their family moved to nearby Boxford. The earliest record I know of regarding their life in Boxford is February 28, 1772. The Selectmen of Boxford voted the lying out of a road "to Benjamin Dwinell's fence".[37] This was a road to the Topsfield line. There are other references to various members of the Dwinell family living in this southeast corner of Boxford near the Topsfield line.

The existence of the armed militia would act as a significant catalyst for revolution as matters matured. Life continued for Benjamin and Mary in Boxford. Mary was listed as a member of the First Church of Boxford in South Boxford in 1777.

The historian, Howard Zinn, has stated "The American victory over the British army was made possible by the existence of an already-armed people. Just about every white male had a gun, and could shoot. The Revolutionary leadership distrusted the mobs of poor. But they knew the Revolution had no appeal to slaves and Indians. They would have to woo the armed white population."[38] Thus, the local militia became a strong political force on the side of the revolutionists.

A military condition created by the British would prove to be part of their undoing. The militia of the Massachusetts Bay Colony and the other colonies fought much of the Colonial Wars under the leadership of the British Regular army but under the direct control of Provincial officers until the 1757 consolidation. As you read the rolls of the Provincial officers of the Seven Years' War leading Provincial companies and regiments, you see these same names in leadership roles in the army of the American revolutionists as they inherit the Provincial militia organization. Benjamin Dwinell was part of that militia organization.

As a member of the Boxford militia, Benjamin was to be involved, yet again, in conflict. As a veteran of the campaigns at Louisbourg in 1745 and Fort William Henry and Crown Point from 1755 to 1757, Benjamin was a valuable member of the cadre of militia who marched toward Concord on April 19, 1775. He was under the command of Captain Jacob Gould. Benjamin would march toward the Concord Bridge and would come within five miles of the battle.[39]

The roads going east to west toward Concord and Lexington were not as well developed as roads coming from the north or the south. The multi-pronged approach on Concord and Lexington would be an effective action against the British. Other units would arrive at Concord and Lexington first as the battle began.

Benjamin's company would chase the British toward Boston as the British retreated to the safety of their principal city. Along the way, Benjamin's unit as well as other units chasing the British would encounter loyalists to the British position. The loyalist was a Massachusetts Bay colonist who chose not to be a revolutionist. On April 19, 1775, those loyalists who found themselves on the roads leading from Lexington and Concord toward Boston were in a dangerous situation. They along with the British soldiers were rushing to seek refuge in Boston. The loyalists, or Tories as they were also called, suffered considerable indignities as the revolution approached. Some Tories were even tarred and feathered. The revolutionists were quite adroit at seeking out and identifying these people, since the organization of communities was so cohesive.

Later, Benjamin would serve in New York.[40] It was common in the Revolutionary War as it was in the Colonial Wars for men to serve for short periods of time. There were farms to tend and a community to run. He had marched on Concord and continued chasing the English toward Boston. He then returned to Boxford to serve in the militia again.

Later in 1777, Benjamin would move to Keene, New Hampshire. His sons Jonathan and Thomas had gone before him, ostensibly to set up a homestead and a farm. In 1771 it was observed that there many incidents in the Massachusetts Bay Colony estate land inventories in probate of "worn land."[41] The colonists had been working the land since 1620; perhaps Benjamin was motivated to seek better land for farming.

Benjamin settled in the northwestern part of Keene on the way to the Fort at Number Four. The Fort at Number Four had been an important outpost on the edge of the wilderness during the Colonial Wars. The farmers of Keene would till the soil with guns at the ready for the predictable Indian raids. The Indian raids were an important element of the French military strategy during the era of the Colonial Wars. Benjamin was well aware of this history.

The English were a threat in upstate New York. If they were to win at Ticonderoga and Saratoga, New England would be cut off. It may seem that Keene,

New Hampshire would have been protected by the existence of Vermont. This protection was not an important element.

Vermont at this point in history was a republic. It had been designated as the New Hampshire Grants during the Colonial era. In 1777, Vermont was very sparsely settled. The English would have no difficulty crossing southern Vermont to get to Keene. At thirty or more miles per day, it would take only three or four days to cross east from New York. The Battle of Ticonderoga would be an important event for the residents of Keene, including Benjamin and Mary. The British had to be stopped at Ticonderoga to avoid cutting off New Hampshire and Massachusetts.

Benjamin and Mary lived together in Keene until 1805 when Benjamin passed away. He was 78 years of age when he died. He is buried in a cemetery called the Court Street Burial Grounds near his home. The Sons of the American Revolution honor Benjamin with a marker designating his participation in the Revolution. Benjamin had an interesting military career.

It seems that a major part of his life was involved in the preparation for war or participating in war. Yet, he was a country farmer who appeared to be successful in his role. He raised ten children and appeared to have lived a successful life.

Benjamin lived through an important era in American History. Even as he moved to Keene and looked forward to life as a farmer in his later years, there was turmoil and conflict as a new country continued to be fought for and, finally, was born. The diplomatic problems with the British would result in the War of 1812 seven years after Benjamin's death. Life was hard in the hinterlands of New England, but Benjamin was accustomed to this life.

At age 19 he had sailed to Louisbourg to help capture the huge fortress for the English. He had been a member of the Topsfield militia and had trained and been available for war on behalf of the British. His service at Fort William Henry and Crown Point had seen him face the French and the Indians knowing that the Indians were ready to fight a savage war as manipulated by the French and against the land acquisitiveness of the English.

He had returned to Topsfield and then to Boxford expecting peace but becoming increasingly involved in revolutionary activity and ultimately war. He would see his sons go off to war as he joined them at age 49 when he marched toward Concord. He would then move to the edge of the frontier in Keene, New Hampshire, where war appeared nearby again.

His was a typical Dwinell experience in the life of this family from approximately 1660 to 1805. Each of the players in this historical drama had been ready to serve their community, their region and their country. They had been exploited by their mother country and, in Benjamin's case, saw their fellow colonists resort to revolt and revolution. The independent nature of the colonist would now manifest itself in the independent nature of the citizen of a new nation. The Dwinell family would continue to grow as the nation grew. Benjamin Dwinell did his part to create the positive environment and heritage of the Dwinell family members who would be his descendents in the years to come.

4

Thomas, the Minuteman

o o o o o o o o o o o o o o o o o o o o o o o o o o o o o o o o

"What! Ten thousand peasants keep five thousand King's troops
shut up? Well, let us get in, and we'll soon find elbowroom."

—*British Major General John Burgoyne*

"Let it rise, till it meet the sun in his coming, let the earliest light
of the morning gild it, and parting day linger and play on its sum-
mit."

—*Daniel Webster at the Dedication of the Bunker Hill
Monument*

Thomas Dwinell was the second son of Benjamin Dwinell. He was born on
October 27, 1752, in Topsfield, Massachusetts, on his grandfather's farm. Thomas is my great, great, great grandfather. Including Thomas, Benjamin had four
sons and six daughters.[1]

Thomas' father, Benjamin went on the Crown Point Expedition when Thomas was about three and one-half years old. The society that Thomas came into
was an English colony and the Provincial soldiers, like his father, who served
England, were proud to do so. Their pride in giving service to England was vested
in their feeling that they were English subjects. They fully expected to retain the
rights of English subjects.

There were other members of the Dwinell family in both Topsfield and Boxford who were serving the English in military service. Thomas' uncle, Michael II,
had given his life to the English cause at Quebec on the Eastern Frontier.

The earliest record thus available of Thomas moving to Boxford was February
28, 1772. The records of the selectmen's meeting in Boxford of that date indicate
the lying out of a road "to Benjamin Dwinell's fence ... a road to the Topsfield

line."[2] It is reasonable to assume that Benjamin and his family had moved to Boxford at about this time. Box ford records show that there were other members of the Dwinell clan living in the southeast corner of Boxford near the Topsfield line at about this point in history.[3]

As the Colonial Wars came to an end in the early 1760s, the political climate in the Massachusetts Bay Colony was beginning to change. The demands of the British were interfaced with the increased confidence of the colonists. The citizens of the Massachusetts Bay Colony considered themselves to be British subjects but also Americans.[4] After all, they had carved out a civilization beginning in 1620, for the Pilgrims, and 1630, for the Puritan settlers. These people had just won a war, virtually alone. Although there was a British command presence, the Provincial soldiers had carried the bulk of the military load. Beyond war, these people had lived in relative freedom. Until this point in history, the British left the colonists virtually alone to manage their self-sufficient society. But, now, the British needed funds to finance their continued conflict with France on the European continent. The colonists in America did not feel that it was their war.

All English peoples believed in the rule of law.[5] Not only was the rule of law and most of the basic freedoms Americans enjoy today part of British law, it was also part of the philosophy accepted by most thinking people. The American colonist was a British subject. Since the colonists were under the legal umbrella of Great Britain, they felt that they enjoyed the same legal privileges of a citizen of England. After winning a war for the mother country, the citizens of the Massachusetts Bay Colony felt that they were equal to their fellow English subjects who happened to live in Great Britain. The English leaders would have other ideas.

The Stamp Act was the first of several measures instituted by the English to raise revenue and to gain control of the economics and politics of their American colony. As they did with the Stamp Act, Americans would react as other measures were passed by the English Parliament that would affect the colonies.

The historian, Samuel Eliot Morison, places the matter in a clearer context. "British subjects in America, excepting of course the Negroes, were then the freest people in the world, and in many respects more free than anyone today. They argued and then fought, not to obtain freedom but to confirm the freedom they already had or claimed."[6] Prior to 1763, the Americans had an essential home rule mechanism in place. The English accepted the self-governing features of these colonies as long as England felt that control was vested in the mother country. There appeared to be a mutual agreement to maintain the status quo. Step by step, the British would change this status quo condition.

In 1760, William Pitt, the British Prime Minister, ordered that the Sugar Act of 1733[7] be strictly enforced. The American colonies had been indulging in a variety of forms of triangular trade with the Caribbean Island nations and France as well as Spain since the late 1600s. Although controls were in place to ban this practice, these controls were not enforced. England was willing to look the other way, until 1760.

Triangular trade was an attempt to obtain trade revenue for the Massachusetts Bay Colony. The acquisition of potential slaves from Africa would start the process. These slaves would be traded to merchants in the West Indies for sugar. The sugar would then be used to create rum in the Massachusetts Bay Colony. The value-added process of creating the rum would enhance the economy of the Massachusetts Bay Colony. Until 1760, the British let this happen despite the presence of the Sugar Act of 1733.[8]

The merchant class of the Massachusetts Bay Colony found a way to accommodate the Sugar Act enforcement. Like any producer-level tax, the imposition of the tax could be passed on as a price increase. As previously explained, the Stamp Act had an effect on everyone. The enforcement of the Sugar Act had its effect directly on the merchant class and only indirectly on the small-town farmer.

The Revenue Act of 1764 was a measure designed to raise revenue for England.[9] This act directly taxed the importation of a long list of luxury products the colonists were accustomed to receiving in trade. The colonists felt that this measure was passed without their consent or input. They felt that this was a violation of the spirit of English law. As we all know from our study of history, the later tax on an additional variety of imports, including tea, was the last straw. The colonists reacted with the now famous Boston Tea Party.[10]

Acts designed to control deliberative assembly; the operation of the courts and other restrictive measures would provide a Colonial reaction. The English decision to maintain a garrison of 10,000 Regular Army troops in Boston added to the turmoil.[11] The Quartering Act made the presence of these 10,000 troops even more invasive. The Act created an atmosphere that made it mandatory to allow British soldiers to live in the homes of some of the colonists.[12]

There was a tradition that the English had to contend with. Farmers were accustomed to the practice of driving their produce to the seaport market to trade for rum and groceries. Every seaport had a rough working-class component of competent laborers who could be organized. Also, the merchant class who were accustomed to a comfortable status quo would have a reaction of their own. These disparate societal elements were to coalesce.[13]

There is a custom in the legislative arena known as the caucus. Legislators of like interest "caucus" to arrive at a strategy to effectively win their point. Samuel Eliot Morison points out that this word had its derivation with the caulkers who worked at the ports. These caulkers along with their fellow dockworkers could "caucus" to invent curious schemes to keep the British authorities working—and wondering. [14]

There were methods in place to help with this organization. Communities were accustomed to meeting in congregations to practice their religion but also to run their town government. Typically, the colonists would use their meeting-house which also served as the community church. This community mechanism would help the Patriots to organize as matters came to a head.

Many leaders would emerge. The historian, David McCullough, would quote John Adams who said, "The true source of our suffering has been our timidity. We have been afraid to think ... Let us dare to read, think, speak, and write ... Let it be known that British liberties are not the grants of princes or parliaments ... that many of our rights are inherent and essential, agreed on as maxims and established as preliminaries, even before Parliament existed.... Let us read and recollect and impress upon our souls the views and ends of our more immediate forefathers, in exchanging their native country for a dreary, inhospitable wilderness...." [15]

Perhaps Thomas Dwinell could remember family stories of the dreary wilderness his great grandfather Michael, Sr. experienced in the 1660s in Topsfield. These Americans who had enjoyed freedom as a seeming reward for their struggles to create a society were not happy. John Adams wanted them to react.

John Adams was truly a great leader even before the revolution took place. There would be other leaders, many in the small towns of the Massachusetts Bay Colony as well as the small towns in the rest of the thirteen colonies.

The colonists did think and they were not timid. When the trade laws were instituted, the colonists would not buy imports, specifically from England. There were Loyalists among the rebel thinkers. These Loyalists were loyal to the English point of view and the leadership of Parliament. There would be an increasing, sometimes violent, reaction to the influence and expressed view of the Loyalists, often referred to as Tories. [16]

The existence of loyalists, or Tories, created a hardship for the rebels, or Patriots. Sometimes, families were split. Lifelong friendships ended. And good neighbors became enemies. Political and mob pressure was brought to bear upon judges to listen to the Patriot's point of view as an offset to the attempts of the British to appoint their own judges and control the actions of these newly appointed judges. When the courts would not conform to the rebel's wishes, the courts were essentially shut down.[17] Across Massachusetts and other parts of America, British demands were met by organized anarchy.

One example of British coercion that has its contemporary counterpart in the United States is the Admiralty Courts. In this instance, cases would be tried before English judges in English courts where the colonists failed to have jurisdiction. There is some controversy today regarding the trying of alleged terrorists in military and other tribunals where some of the basic rights of an American citizen are not an issue. In contemporary America, these cases are tried outside of the United States court system.

The revolutionists reacted to what they felt was an intrusion of their rights as English subjects. This revolutionary behavior as a reaction to the coercive actions of the British was brought about and organized by the creation of the Committees of Correspondence. Organized at the state level, each community would have its local counterpart. As the Revolution approached war, Committees of Safety were formed as well to have a military-planning function.[18]

The tavern would be a natural communication source for both the issuing of information and the receipt of opinion.[19] The tavern would be an alternative to the meeting halls of the town as the informal organization had an opportunity to thrive. The use of the tavern would alleviate the problem of the minister being in a vulnerable position if the meetinghouse were used. The tavern also could serve as a means to exclude the Loyalists.

It was traditional for the colonists to have plenty of rum available in the taverns of the provinces. The now illicit triangular trade with the West Indies assured a supply. Unlike the British who controlled the colonies by edict, the opinions of the people who were to react in an organized manner to these edicts were solicited to determine the prevailing point of views. This practice proved effective. In fact, Ray Raphael points out that the strongest impetus for action came from the small towns rather than the Boston intellectuals or the wealthy Salem and Boston merchants. Many of the ideas came from the central cities. The towns were action-oriented.[20]

One concept that any union organizer knows is that when you advocate a reasonable course of action, the more militant will react. As a leader, you want the people you are representing to react. In the short run, the organizer has a problem. In the long run, this problem is transferred to the adversary.

As matters escalated and as each community organized in concert with the state Committee of Correspondence, a military device created by the British became a valuable Patriot tool. The militia used by the British in the Colonial

Wars was still in place.[21] Thomas' father, Benjamin, was a member of the Boxford militia and would march on Concord as part of a militia regiment, just as he marched on Louisbourg, Crown Point, and helped to build William Henry. The British had trained him and other militia members well.[22]

The militia was composed of men who had families to protect and farms to manage. To a large degree, these men lived on the outskirts of town. It would take time to get them marshaled in an emergency. It was necessary to have a force of men who would be able to be organized more quickly.

The town of Concord, Massachusetts lays claim to the birth of an organization of soldiers known as the Minutemen. On September 26, 1774, the Town of Concord voted "that there be one or more Companys Raised in this Town by Enlistment and that they Chuse their officers out of the Body So inlisted and that Said Company or Companies Stand at a minutes warning in Case of an alarm and when said Company Should be Called for out of Town, in that Case the Town Pay said Company or Companies Reasonable wages for the time they were absent."[23]

In Concord, Minute Men trained twice a week on the town common. They carried their weapons everywhere, "in fields, in shops, even to church." Supplies were obtained or manufactured. The women of the town made the cartridges; hence, the Town was ready. Someone even managed to steal cannon from Boston.[24]

Other towns, including Boxford, organized Minuteman units as well. These units were organized into regiments. These men complemented the militia regiments to form an army. It is important to remember that the logistics of this organized army was planned for the most part before Concord and Lexington.[25] Through the Committee of Safety and local organization, the revolutionists had done their homework.

There was an alert on April 19, 1975. Thomas answered the call as a Minuteman and proceeded on a quick march toward the Concord Bridge. Like his father who was in the militia regiment, he came within five miles of the Concord Bridge.[26] The march from Boxford went through Andover. More men were added at Andover. They then proceeded toward Concord going through Billerica on the way. It took awhile to make this march. These two regiments with others then proceeded to chase the British toward Boston as far as Cambridge. The Minuteman regiments then joined General William Heath at Charlestown Neck. The Minuteman regiment that Thomas was part of then becomes part of the force that fought at the Battle of Bunker Hill.[27]

At this point in history, Boston was a relatively small piece of land that would be an island except for two small necks joining the mainland. Charlestown Neck was the most northern small body of land joining the peninsula of Charlestown to the town of Cambridge close to the Somerville town line. Roxbury Neck (Often called Boston Neck or Dorchester Neck) joined the mainland area of Roxbury to Boston proper in an area just past the Boston Common.

Charlestown Neck was near the present day Sullivan Square in Charlestown while Roxbury Neck was near Tremont Street south of the Boston Common. Bunker Hill is in Charlestown as a part of Boston. The neck is to the north of Charlestown as is the Mystic River. The Charles River separates the Village of Charlestown from Boston proper. This rough geographic orientation would help one to understand the logistics of the coming Battle. As you consider the battle, think of Charlestown as a peninsula joined to the mainland by a very narrow Charlestown Neck. If you were familiar with the Sullivan Square area as it is today, you would realize that the land at this point is no longer narrow. Much of the area has been filled in.

As General Galvin's account of the aftermath of the Battle of Lexington and Concord indicates, Thomas, as part of Colonel Frye's regiment, was involved in the Battle of Bunker Hill.[28] His application for a Revolutionary War Pension indicates that he "assisted in building fortifications on Bunker Hill the night before the battle; was in the fight afterwards." His brother, Jonathan, testified in the deposition in the application for the pension that Jonathan had served with his brother. This statement that he assisted in building the fortifications and was in the battle is an extreme understatement given the nature of the military situation and the resultant battle.[29] If he were there as he states, there is more to the explanation than just that he assisted in the building and was in the fight.

The stage for the battle should be set, first. For that step, we need to go back to Cambridge and to Harvard College.

Thomas was in Colonel James Frye's Regiment. Since the colonel was ill on the evening of June 16, 1775, Thomas was under the command of Lieutenant Colonel James Brickett.

On the evening of June 16, 1775, the Stoughton, Harvard and Massachusetts Halls of Harvard College were overflowing with a rather disreputable group of seemingly disorganized and non-uniform group of men who were to be the invading force of a great battle.[30] In a fashion uncharacteristic for a military force, the uniforms of these men were unimpressive. The armament they employed was not at all uniform. The number of different types of firearms almost matched the number of men involved.

The conditions of their encampment were deplorable and their prediction for success from any unbiased observer would be bleak. This rag tag group of rebels was about to take on three regiments of the British Army and seven ships of the British Navy. The British Army was the greatest fighting force in the world at this point in history. The British Navy had dominated the waters of Western Europe for centuries. Thomas was among this upstart group of rebels who would engage the greatest military power on earth.

Richard Ketchum in his *The Battle for Bunker Hill*, has stated "Whatever else the men in the ranks may have guessed about their assignment, it seems certain that none knew their objective. Peter Brown, a young company clerk in Colonel Prescott's regiment, made that plain when he wrote his mother nine days later. 'Frydy the 16th of June' he reported, 'we were ordered to parade at 6 o'clock with one day's provisions and blankets ready for a march somewhere, but we did not know where. So we readly and cheerfully obeyed, the whole that was called for, which was these three, Col. Prescott's, Fry's, and Nickson's regiments....' (He was confused—it was Bridge's, not Nixon's, regiment that reported fir duty that night.)[31] Relative to Peter Brown's observation, one of the problems that the commanders would have as the battle ultimately begun is that these inexperienced men did not necessarily bring enough food with them. In the toughest and most rigorous portion of the battle the next day after having worked all night, these men were exhausted and desperately in need of food.[32] These were undisciplined soldiers who lacked the experience of the British army. Minutemen were the young men of the community who had not fought for the British twenty years before. Although undisciplined, they were enthusiastic and willing to carry out orders. They understood the cause and were ready to fight for it.

As the assembly at Harvard got ready to proceed, Colonel Gridley had a work crew collecting books from the library. One has to wonder how many of these soldiers could read anything, let alone the esoteric tomes of the Harvard College Library. Colonel Gridley's battalion was busy as well with their six fieldpieces and guns taken from the schooner "Diana". Captain Foster began loading the wagons with entrenching tools. The books appear incongruous to the scene unless as camouflage among the military hardware.[33]

When ordered, the men then marched north for a short distance to Cambridge Common. They assembled just east of what is now Brattle Street, known then as Tory Row. The group had other business than a preoccupation with the wealthy Loyalists. The march was soon to begin to the east toward the Inman Farm, Lechemere's Point and Charlestown Neck. Their ultimate goal was Bunker Hill, or was it?[34]

The orders read "Whereas, it appears of Importance to the Safety of this Colony, that possession of the Hill, called Bunker's Hill, in Charlestown, be securely kept and defended; and also some one hill or hills on Dorchester Neck be likewise Secured. Therefore, Resolved, Unanimously, that it be recommended to the Council of War, that the abovementioned Bunker's Hill be maintained, by sufficient force being posted there, and as the particular situation of Dorchester Neck is unknown to this Committee, they advise that the Council of War take and pursue such steps respecting the Same, as to them shall appear to be for the Security of this Colony."[35]

These orders notwithstanding, when the expedition reached Charlestown Neck, there was a conference among the regimental officers. The outgrowth of this conference was to choose Breed's Hill to defend. As military experts have studied the Battle of Bunker Hill through the centuries, this conference and the ultimate decision engenders considerable conversation and controversy. Nevertheless, the several regiments marched toward Breed's Hill. Breed's Hill is the smaller of the two hills and is near the southernmost point of Charlestown near the Charles River.

The regiments commanded by these three colonels set out to build the fortifications on the top of Breed's Hill. The task began as darkness fell. One thousand men began to dig. Thomas was one of these men.

Colonel Gridley was an engineer who knew how to accomplish this task. Yet, he did not know how these men could accomplish this task with the British Army in Boston at the base of the hill and across the Charles and seven ships of the British Navy in the Charles River below to the south and to the west.[36]

Nearly all of these men were farmers. They knew how to dig and they knew how to erect structures. The danger was obvious and the realization that daylight would come all too soon was equally apparent. As matters turned out, it was necessary for these men to keep working even when the British knew they were there and had begun firing their cannon. In one of the first few volleys, a soldier was beheaded; the men kept working. To keep the men working, Colonel Prescott climbed the newly formed wall on the southern point of Breed's Hill right at the point where the fatal volley had landed and strode up and down the wall in full view of the British gunboats as he urged his men. Given his brave, or foolhardy, actions, how could Thomas have refused to keep digging?

The battle continued throughout the day as the British began to mobilize for the attack. The British landed at Moulton's Point, the southeast point of Charlestown, at 1:00 p.m. Combat had begun.

The first attack was at 3:30 p.m. The rebels repelled the first attack. There would be two more attacks at 4:00 and at 4:30 p.m. the last onslaught necessitated a retreat back toward Charlestown Neck and to the safety of Cambridge. By this time Colonel Stark's New Hampshire Regiment had recently arrived. Colonel Stark's regiment aided the retreat with covering fire. Colonel Stark and his men held their ground despite the existence of fire from the ships in the western part of the Charles River.[37]

This battle was a military success despite the retreat of the Patriots. The British suffered large losses and came to the realization that the Patriots were to be a potent force.

Thomas would have volunteered to be a Minuteman. In his case he had enlisted in April 1775, for eight months.[38] After the Battle for Bunker Hill, he was stationed at Cambridge until the end of his enlistment. He then immediately re enlisted for a period of two months. This first tour of duty in Massachusetts was from April 1775, until February 1776. Thomas does not mention any remarkable battle record after the action he participated in at Bunker Hill. [39]

Thomas returned home to Boxford, Massachusetts, to make preparations to move to Keene, New Hampshire. He moved to Keene, New Hampshire, sometime during 1776. His father would join him during 1777.[40] Soon after March 14, 1776, Thomas signed a document with his fellow townspeople of Keene to pledge allegiance to the United Colonies.[41] A resolution was passed in the Colonial Congress on that March date. Soon thereafter at a selectmen's meeting the pledge was administered. Other business took place on April 23, 1776. Although I do not have a date for the pledge document, the April 23 reference suggests a date near to this day.

There were continuing appeals for help at Fort Ticonderoga in New York. On May 3, the New Hampshire State committee of safety ordered each of three colonels to form militia units to answer this call.[42] Thomas became part of Captain Howlett's company of Keene.

British General Burgoyne had a plan for separating New England from the rest of the colonies. During the French and Indian War, the French and the English had built a series of forts down the waterways of Lake Champlain and Lake George in New York. The general planned to use these forts. He also planned to move up the Hudson River from New York City toward Albany and Lake George. This was a plan that would be very threatening to Keene, New Hampshire.

Even though the then Republic of Vermont had been settled for several decades, the areas in central and southern Vermont were only sparsely settled.

Western Massachusetts could be described in the same fashion. Keene, New Hampshire is in southwestern New Hampshire only a few miles east of the Connecticut River. There were a few forts between Keene and New York but hardly the major forts such as Ticonderoga and Saratoga. Keene needed to be defended, as did Ticonderoga. The militia of Keene was needed.

Although sparsely populated and somewhat of a political afterthought between New York and New Hampshire, the people of Vermont had reason to be a potent force. Under the leadership of Ethan Allen, they had made a contribution in the Colonial Wars. Now, they made a contribution at Ticonderoga. Keene would be indebted to Allen for this effort.

In late June 1776, a militia group began its march toward Ticonderoga. Thomas would march under the command of Captain Howlett.[43] This group was called back to Keene but was to marshal again. Altogether, there would be four different alarms that these men would have to honor. Thomas Dwinell was involved in this process as he once again answered the call.[44]

The people of Keene were accustomed to alarms. They lived only fifteen or twenty miles southeast of the Fort at Number Four. Twenty years earlier they were aware of Indian raids at the fort. Keene farmers were used to being ready for attack. They would once again plow their fields with rifles at the ready.

Thomas does not mention the Ticonderoga engagement in his application for a Revolutionary War pension. Apparently, his father, Benjamin, did not apply for a pension either even though he had Revolutionary War militia experience. It would appear that the role of the militia was to answer temporary alarms. Thomas applied for the pension, evidently, based on his length of service as an enlistee in the Regular Army in Massachusetts. It was typical in the Revolutionary War for soldiers to maintain a normal life between expeditions. The daily routine of private life would be carried out as well as possible.

Despite the war, Thomas and his brother, Jonathan, appear to have been successful in Keene. The Dwinell gristmill was erected on Willson's pond in 1776.[45] Typical of the era, two soldiers, Thomas and his brother Jonathan, were ready to defend their country maintain their life and run their grist mill as they stood ready for war.

As the war came to a conclusion, the citizen-soldiers returned to devote full time to their families and their work. Thomas and Jonathan had a gristmill to run a farm to manage and contract work to do in the community.[46]

Meanwhile, there was a nation to build. We had won a war; now the work would begin. The British government did not leave automatically, especially in

New Hampshire.[47] It was necessary to displace the British presence in New Hampshire legally.

The process of building a constitution, electing a president, forming a government and starting a nation was a challenge that would involve the citizens of the thirteen colonies. However, in the hinterlands there was a life to lead. Even so, the process was democratic. There would be a local involvement. Even though farmers worked from dawn to nightfall, they would be involved in the process of building a nation just as the political leaders would in the several new states.

Thomas would perform various farm-laboring tasks as life continued. He occupied a home on Whyman Road in 1787.[48] He then bought a farm in 1805.[49] This farm was in the northwest area of Keene near the north line. Keene was still a rural community. There was a bounty on wolves and other wildlife was apparent.[50] Family tradition tells us that Thomas' brother in law, Ichabod, had the experience of being hugged by a bear—twice. He carried the scars of these incidents for a lifetime. Author's note: My source did not indicate if it were the same bear. Ichabod was the brother of Thomas' wife, Sarah Hammond Dwinell.[51] I have a handwritten account of family stories that includes this incident.

This incident indicates that southern New Hampshire was still quite rural as it is today. Thomas was to continue to live as a farmer and a gristmill operator in this rural community until his death in 1837.[52] In 1782, "Thomas Dwinell raised his large house frame on the tract of land between Governor Archer's and S. Ellis's land."[53] The barn had been raised on July 10, 1781. For a farmer of that era, the barn would be more important than the house.

Thomas was essentially a farmer and a farm laborer who had the enterprise to run a gristmill with his brother, Jonathan, and his father. Like so many Americans, necessity had provided him with a military career. He had served and came home to Keene to live his life and manage his farm and his mill. He and Sarah would have ten children. Thomas had an active life in a critical era in our history.

It is easy to say that Thomas came home after the war and lived with Sarah happily ever after. But with the cessation of most wars, there were problems beyond the formation of a government. The historian of Vermont and New Hampshire, Ralph Nading Hill, has stated "Money depreciated and an army of lawyers tramped up and down the valleys serving writs."[54] The war was won; the peace needed to be won as well.

Not only was Great Britain strong militarily, they also were very sophisticated diplomatically and had the strongest economy in Europe. America still depended upon England for trade goods. The strong emergent capitalist economy of

England would continue to be a powerful force and a threat to American freedom. A depreciated currency is always a threat to a farmer, particularly a farmer who manages a gristmill dependent on the prosperity of other farmers. Evidently, Thomas survived this threat and managed to build a life for his family in Keene.

Thomas had been born near the end of the French and Indian War when the militia, including his father, had been treated so badly by the British Regular Army commanders. He grew up in an atmosphere of turmoil seeing his father active in the militia. Then, he became a young soldier as a Minuteman from Boxford, Massachusetts. He had marched on Concord and remained in military service long enough to fight in the Battle for Bunker Hill and to be part of a force ready to serve for several months thereafter. He had set out to join his brother to Keene, New Hampshire to start a new life. Soon thereafter, his father and mother would follow Jonathan and Thomas to Keene. Then, he found himself and his fellow townsmen involved in the threat posed by the Battle for Ticonderoga. Once again, his life as a young farmer was threatened. Yet, he and his family prevailed. Thomas passed away on March 31, 1836. He was 83 years of age when he died.

He is buried in the Ash Swamp Cemetery in the western part of Keene. Like his father, Benjamin, there is a Sons of the American Revolution marker designating his grave as a Patriot burial site.

Thomas continued the military heritage begun by his father and his uncles in the Colonial Wars. He also continued the heritage of the land and of community service that Michael, Sr., had started two centuries earlier.

Thomas had purchased land in Glover, Vermont, and then sold it to his son, Solomon. The tradition of the land was preserved. The Dwinell tradition of land ownership and farming continued in Vermont by Joseph, Dwight and Rolland as the nineteenth century went by. This tradition was to be changed as the ninth generation emerged in the twentieth century. The college-educated ninth generation would present a different tradition for their descendants to follow. The tenth generation continued this success

They have in their genes the advantages of a rural environment. The independence of the Vermont and the Colonial experience is evident. It is bolstered by the sophistication of a modern environment. The proud legacy of Thomas and his father, Benjamin made this possible. Without men like these two members of the Dwinell family the freedom we know today would not exist.

Thomas' sons would move to Vermont. My great, great grandfather, Solomon, would be one of these sons. We will meet him in the next chapter. Thomas evidently went to Glover, Vermont, to obtain farm land for his sons following the tradition of the farm life being sustained through the generation. Once again the Dwinell family decided to explore a new life in an even more rural region than their previous abode as the result of Thomas' investigation of land acquisition possibilities in Glover, my great, great grandfather started the Vermont legacy for the Dwinell family.

5

Vermont Legacy

o o o o o o o o o o o o o o o o o o o o o o o o o o o o o o o o

"... a district where, ... the climate is eight months winter, and four months of darned late in the fall ... with more than half of its land tip-tilted ..."

—Dorothy Canfield Fisher

One year after "eighteen hundred and damned near froze to death" a man named Solomon Dwinell acquired Lot C 83, 60 Acres, for $270[1] in Glover, Vermont. 1816 was quite a year in the state of Vermont. "Growing crops were covered with snow. Cold and snow killed the leaves of the trees, birds perished by the hundreds. Harvests were light. Corn sold at $2.00 a bushel, wheat at $4.00."[2] Compare these prices with the acquisition of $270 for Solomon's total farm.

This was rugged country and rather sparsely populated. Solomon settled just south of Keene Corner, a section of Glover inhabited by people who had come from Keene, New Hampshire.[3] This deed indicates that he had purchased his lot from Thomas Dwinell, I can assume that this was his father. His brother's name was Thomas H. Dwinell. Perhaps his father purchased the land for his son from those former Keene residents who relocated to Keene Corner.

Glover had been organized as a community in 1798. The community possessed 23,040 acres that the organizers divided into 144 lots of 160 acres each.[4] Solomon purchased one part of one of these lots. Solomon, his wife Mary, and his son, Albert, came from Keene, New Hampshire. It is believed that Solomon arrived in March of 1818.[5] This arrival date means that Solomon and his family traveled under wintry conditions. In many respects, this time of year would have been the best time to travel. The snow on the ground would have allowed sleds to be used. As they headed north, they could have used the frozen Connecticut River to make sled traffic easier. Although forests were thinning in southern New

England, the virgin forests of the north would have made travel through the woods a difficult task. They would have had to go through the woods from the area near the present city of St. Johnsbury, Vermont, to Glover. It would be easier in the woods in the winter. The lack of leaves would have provided some visibility. Also, the frozen ground of the winter would have made travel easier than the mud to be encountered in the spring.

If they had chosen warmer weather conditions to travel this road, they would have had a problem. They could not have used the river unless they wanted to row upstream, so they would go over the land. This would not have been an asphalt road. Asphalt was not used until almost a century later. These roads were often referred to as "corduroy roads" because of the nature of their construction. Logs were set into the road parallel to the length of the road in swampy areas to allow carts to ford these spots. This condition would provide an uncomfortable ride and present a difficult task for the person pulling the load if oxen were not available. Even these rudimentary roads would not have been available except near substantial towns.

There had been many stories about the hardships of leaving southern New England for the wilds of the north. Many of the pioneers had to "back" all of their possessions. This backing process means that you would carry everything that your family owned literally on their back. The family had to eat along the way. Sometimes a man would have to walk for fifty miles to find the necessary game.

When conventional food was not available, it would be necessary for the family to live on browse, the twigs and bark of the trees. The Indians had observed that this habit kept the deer alive, so the impoverished Indian would survive on browse. The pioneer learned that this habit was a valuable survival tool.[6]

People had been coming to Vermont for several decades. Some people came to have a religious life somewhat more relaxed than the rigorous life of the Puritan. Many people left as the trees were in shorter supply to the south. People had been leaving Connecticut, Massachusetts and southern New Hampshire because of diminishing resources including animal life in southern New England.[7]

The lot of Solomon's farm was Lot 83. It was near the top of a rise that today is known as Sheffield Heights. Lot 84 is right at the border between Glover and the next town of Sheffield. Each of these lots is on the western side of the road. These lots overlook a wide vista that includes Mount Mansfield on the horizon to the west, southwest. This picturesque location is where Solomon built his log cabin and began life in the Northeast Kingdom of Vermont. In her genealogical notes, Sarah Dwinell Stebbins has said that the chimney that Solomon erected in his log cabin was so large that one could lie on the floor and see the stars through its opening.[8]

Solomon Dwinell was the fifth child and second son of Thomas and Sarah Dwinell. He was born on July 3, 1792, in Keene, New Hampshire.[9] Solomon married Mary Brown in 1816. Their first son, Albert, was born that first year.[10] At the time that Solomon and Mary set out to travel to Glover, Albert was five months old.

The migration of farmers to Vermont had a long history that began in the middle of the eighteenth century. There were many stories of the hardships of families that moved from Connecticut and Western Massachusetts to Vermont for several reasons including the need for virgin farmland. There was an abundance of land in Vermont in the eighteenth century and an abundance of a wild life population. The English government would provide a grant of land for anyone who would agree to clear the land and prepare it for farming.[11]

Between New Hampshire and New York, it was a forbidding land, hilly, mountainous and cold. The land-grant incentives instituted by the English provided the impetus for people to go there, and some people enjoyed the freedom and the opportunity to begin a new life. This settlement of Vermont in the 1700s did not go quite as far north as Glover. The settlement of Glover began in the 1790s and the town began to be organized in 1793 to 1798.[12]

There are many stories that tell of the hardships of those early settlers of Vermont. Relevant to the story of Solomon's journey to Glover with his family is the oft-repeated story of Seth Hubbell. Hubbell migrated from southern Connecticut to Wolcott, Vermont, in 1789. Wolcott is about 25 miles southwest of Glover. As his journey continued, one of his oxen "gave out", and the other oxen could not function without his companion. Seth talks of "backing" his family goods meaning he played the role of pack animal across the trail. The trail was a marked trail through the woods. If the marking were by Indians, the trail would be barely discernible to the Colonists, and perhaps to Seth.

I am not aware of any significant place in history that the name Seth Hubbell occupies. His story is a typical experience that others before and after him replicated. The pioneers who went to northern Vermont from southern areas were ordinary people. Their lives are worth recounting to denote these experiences as real. To me Seth Hubbell is one of these people.

There was an expression used by the pioneers called "pinching time" which meant that your stomach literally pinched as you experienced hunger. Try eating twigs for a week while working eight to ten hours a day pulling a sled with everything you own together with your wife and an infant son on board. Then, observe the feeling in your stomach.

Once in Vermont, there was land to be cleared. Farmers like Seth Hubbell would clear the land burning the stumps. The ashes from the resultant fire had an economic value as potash. In fact, for most of the era of Vermont settlement in the eighteenth century, potash served as a medium of exchange as well as a valuable export product to Europe to be used in the wool industry. Conventional money was not used outside of the central trading centers of the Colonies.[13] By the time Solomon came to Glover the potash trade with Europe had ended and the United States had the beginnings of a monetary system. The job of clearing land was there, and farmers needed to be extremely careful in their use of cash.

As Solomon found his way to this frontier environment, the rapidly emerging capitalistic environment of England was thriving. The capitalists of London were reaping financial reward. One such financial capitalist was an economist named David Ricardo, a London stockbroker. He had devised an impeccable set of theories on foreign trade and on the concepts of productivity still in use today. He contended that a country with a favorable stock of capital utilized well could prosper if they indulged in free trade to the absolute and comparative advantage of the nation in question, England.

His marginal productivity analysis introduced the concept of the precise measurement of production. The central question of Ricardo's reasoning would be what quantity of output would result from the next quantity of input. The logical outcome of this theory would be that maximum benefit would occur precisely when the marginal increment of output exactly equaled the marginal increment of input. The examples of the results of his theories were abundant and his arguments could not be disputed. In fact, his reasoning is still a central part of microeconomic reasoning. This theory helps explain the relative measure of efficiency in a single farm environment.

Meanwhile, a country minister far from the London marketplace had another view. The good reverend, Thomas Malthus, saw that there would be a geometric increase in the numbers of people in the world (1, 2, 4, 8, 16 …) while the production of goods would grow arithmetically (1, 2, 3, 4 …). He contended that the key to the well being of people was their ability to consume. Yet, he believed that there was a finite limit to the productive capacity of the entire world. He further contended that in the long run the ability of all of the people to have an adequate supply of consumption goods was in jeopardy. His reasoning was based on a measure of the total production of the society as a whole rather than the marginal production of one producer at a time.[14] Ricardo and Malthus did not necessarily disagree with one another. They saw the economy from different perspectives.

As matters turned out, it would be a long time before anyone would take Malthus seriously. Although the reasoning behind the Malthusian question is probably what motivated Solomon to move to Vermont, there were Ohio, Indiana, and beyond. Lewis and Clark had told America of a great uncharted continent and the Malthusian pessimism seemed misplaced. Solomon probably did not read the Malthusian literature but seemed happy on his Vermont farm. The Ricardo and Malthus debate raged at just about the time of Solomon's migration.

As matters turned out, the United States did not have to worry about a lack of abundance for some time. We will return to this thesis. Remember, though, the example of lessening farm productivity in Massachusetts and southern New Hampshire may have been the motivating force causing Solomon to leave Keene, New Hampshire, in 1817. Even then we lived in a finite world.

Today as of 1980, Glover is still a very small farm community of 840 people. It is a very pretty town with rolling hills and picturesque farms. The country store is an important community center and the Busy Bee restaurant is the main restaurant in town serving about twelve snuggly-seated customers. There are two or three lakes to make the scene even more pleasing.

One of these lakes no longer exists. It ran away.

A few years before Mary and Solomon arrived with their young son, an incident occurred in Glover. This incident is a story of the land that is common to the people of the Northeast Kingdom. It is a legend but appears to have a basis in fact. There are many versions of the story. This version appears typical.

"On June 6, 1810, the inhabitants of Glover and adjoining towns were interested in the matter. Assembled to the number of about sixty at Keene Corner, and thence proceeded to the northern shore of Long Pond and commenced digging a channel, through which was to flow the water considered necessary for the comfort of those residing on the banks of the Barton River. The channel was commenced about three feet from the waters of the pond and descended to the point where the descent was rapid toward Mud pond. When all was ready the connection with the pond was effected by removing the barrier which had been left, and the water issued through the opening with only moderate force, but to the surprise of the workmen it did not follow the channel dug, but descended into the sand beneath."[15]

The account of this incident goes on to explain that the stream of water had encountered hard pan and quicksand. As a result, a huge torrent of water coursed its way toward Lake Memprhemagog, some twenty miles north via the Barton

River. This is the story of Runaway Pond. As you drive south out of Glover toward Greensborough, Vermont, there is a sign designating the site, as this is a story important to the inhabitants of the area even today. A careful study of this geological phenomenon helps one to understand the nature of the Glover environment.

Solomon appears to have adapted well to this relatively harsh environment. There is a myriad of real estate transactions involving Solomon that caused him to acquire parcels of land throughout the town.[16] Farmers would sell these parcels, even buying back a given parcel years later. It appears that these transactions were to enhance cash flow on the one hand and to acquire tillable land on the other hand.

The family farmer needs to live by a growing cycle involving both livestock and produce. At certain times during the year, the farmer must buy equipment and seeds for growth and food for animals. He needs cash for this purpose. Then, the farmer needs to wait for harvest or for the optimum time to sell livestock. Meanwhile, he and his family must rely on the economic value of dairy cattle and egg producing hens as well as wool bearing sheep to eke out a living. Cash is in short supply. Land is a resource with an economic value, hence the real estate transaction.

Solomon appears to have done well. An 1859 map of Glover shows that Solomon owned a farm near Shadow Lake in the southern part of Glover. His son, Albert, owned a nearby farm near the main road heading south. These farms are on parts of Lots 63 and 64 of the town map. Following Yankee tradition, Solomon had sold part of his holdings to his elder son, Albert.[17] At this point in history, the Dwinell family did not own Lots 83 and 84 but were to reacquire these lots later. Solomon would sell these lots to his son, Joseph.[18] A later map of the town shows that Albert still owned 80 acres of Lot 63. Joseph and his son, Dwight, owned 160 acres of Lots 83 and 84 and Solomon owned 80 acres of Lot 81.[19]

The 1870 census demonstrates the productivity of these farms. To use maple sugar as an example Solomon's farm produced 2,000 pounds of maple sugar while Joseph's farm produced 300 pounds of maple sugar and Albert's farm produced 1,000 pounds of maple sugar. Both Albert and Joseph had farms more suited for the raising of livestock and growing of produce while Solomon's farm was heavily wooded.[20]

Solomon had a very well deserved reputation in Glover for being a successful farmer. He also served in many capacities in town government including the role of selectman. From 1849 until 1859, he served as a Probate Judge in the County

Court.[21] I asked a practicing lawyer how someone could be a judge in 1849 without formal training in the law. He indicated that people tended to read the law and then to practice the profession. This occurred before formal academic and licensing preparation was needed. One well known example of the self-educated lawyer is the story of Abraham Lincoln.

Solomon and Mary had three daughters and two sons. They certainly had an active life in Glover and are mentioned as important elements in the development of the community.[22] They and their family were members in good standing of the Glover Village Congregational Church.[23]

I have an artifact that I feel belonged to Solomon. If so, he represents the generation from further back in time than any other Dwinell member for which I have a specific reminder. My wife, Ann, feels that my contention may be chauvinistic.

When Ann and I visited my cousin, Alice, in Quincy in about 1995, she asked me if I wanted to have "grandfather's clock" to keep as a family heirloom. I accepted the clock. Since all of our children had grown to be thirty something, the risk seemed reasonable.

Assuming this responsibility caused me to visit a clockmaker. He is a specialist in the collection and repair of antique clocks. He told me that I now possessed a Seth Thomas Connecticut Valley Shelf Clock.[24]

He then explained that Seth Thomas believed that every family should own a clock. Using the same marketing principle, Henry Ford would proclaim many decades later that every family should own an automobile. The clockmaker then proceeded to show me why this rather elegant looking antique could be made at a low enough cost for every family to own one of these devices.

He took off the protective plate to show me the small, intricate parts. These parts were made of wood. He told me that these parts were manufactured up and down the Connecticut River Valley in little machine shops. His catalogues indicated that the production of these clocks occurred during the 1830s. This clock manufacturing business was an excellent example of the emergence of capitalism taking place in America. Perhaps this clock could be tied to Solomon. When I ventured this theory to Ann, she suggested that the clock could have belonged to my grandmother's family. She has a point, either way, I have a tie to my great, great grandfather. I don't know how to prove who is right; maybe the Seth Thomas Company has sales records.

I have another specific reference to Solomon from Sarah Dwinell Stebbins. You will recall that she referred to Solomon's fireplace in his first log cabin. Sarah Stebbins indicated in her genealogical notes that when Solomon returned home from work one day at age 80 he proceeded to mow three quarters of an acre on his farm. He then turned and fluffed the hay after dinner. She says that her source is my grandfather, Dwight Dwinell. Solomon appears to have been an able farmer, a valuable community leader and a competent judge as well as a pretty strong farmer, too.

Solomon accomplished the foundation for a-four-generation tenure for our branch of the Dwinell clan in Glover, Vermont. Dwinell Drive is still a dirt road leading off Route 16 on the right as Route 16 heads south toward Greensborough. The Johnson farm lies just beyond the small bridge and beaver dam formed on what I think is the Barton River of Runaway Pond fame. Today, the Johnson family breeds Belgian horses on this farm. This piece of land is the part of Lot 63 that was Solomon's son Albert's farm. Mrs. Johnson indicated to me that there is the foundation of a farmhouse upon the hill at the top of the pasture and into the woods. This foundation may have been the most westerly point of Albert's land, therefore, Albert's home. It may also have been Solomon's home. His land appears to have been farther along Dwinell Drive overlooking Shadow Lake.

Route 122 runs southeast farther north from Dwinell Drive off Route 16. It climbs a hill for about half a mile to the Sheffield town line. This is the area at the top of this hill where Solomon built his first log cabin in 1817. As the years went by, land changed hands. Eventually, Solomon's son, Joseph, and his grandson, Dwight, would own this farm. Solomon passed away on this farm in 1878. He was 86 years of age. He had accomplished a great deal including being the founder of our Vermont heritage.

Solomon Dwinell had five children. Albert was born in Keene, New Hampshire, and was the first child to set up farming on the eastern portion of Lot 63. Albert and Lydia Dwinell had two daughters, Lydia and Ellen, and an adopted son, Watson D. Harkee. We shall talk later about the traditional need for a son on a family farm.

Solomon had three daughters, Cornelia, Mary and Sarah. His third oldest child and youngest son was Joseph. Joseph was born on October 18, 1821. As one looks at the records of Glover, there are three people named Joseph Dwinell. Joseph H. Dwinell is Solomon's brother. The letter H stands for the surname Hammond. Their mother's maiden name was Sarah Hammond. My great grandfather had no middle initial. Evidently he was just plain Joe.

Joseph E. Dwinell is Joseph H. Dwinell's son. [25] My son, Joseph, has an artifact of Joseph E. Dwinell. When I lived in Lowell I realized that we had this artifact. Joseph E. Dwinell had produced the bedroom set used by my parents. The bed of this set is now in my son Joseph's attic. Both of these Dwinells other than my great grandfather were prominent in Glover at the time my great grandfather was running his farm.

It is mentioned in Ira Dwinell's genealogy that both Solomon and Joseph shared Pew Number One in the Glover Congregational Church.[26] They were members in good standing of the church maintaining a long-standing family tradition.

My great grandfather, Joseph, married Ann P. Cook on October 28, 1847 on his 25th birthday. Joseph and Ann were to have two children, Dwight and Irene.[27] Joseph and Ann are my great grandparents. Just before their marriage in 1846, Joseph received 160 acres of land from his father.[28] This purchase was for parts of Lots 83 and 84. The land acquired is on the top of Sheffield Heights in Glover looking over a wide expanse of land and mountains to the southwest all the way to Mount Mansfield. The sales price for this land was $1,000.

The concept of selling land to one's son is a long-standing Yankee tradition. You may recall that Solomon sold the east portion of Lot 63 to his oldest son, Albert, for $800. Older Vermont farmers often were land-rich and cash poor. Later, Joseph would acquire other lots of land in a series of transactions. Farmers continued to buy and sell land to enhance both their respective farms and their cash positions. This sale and purchase of land practice continued in Glover as the nineteenth century progressed.

As you visit a small Vermont town such as Glover, you can get a sense of life on a family farm. My wife, Ann, and I visited Glover twice in the early fall of 2004. The first time was in mid September. We went back during the last week of September. We drove up each time to the Sheffield town line to see Lots 83 and 84. The view was beautiful, particularly when the leaves had turned. We could see the orange-red sugar maple trees, so we learned that some sugaring would still be conducted on the current farm.

The weather was pleasant. It was easy to see the advantages of outdoor life during the temperate summer and early fall in this area. As I looked toward Mount Mansfield, I could imagine the winters. A good deal of weather in Vermont comes from the west. Lots 83 and 84 have a western exposure. Winds would be common and unabated as would sub zero temperatures.

Before driving up Route 122 to Sheffield Heights, we had lunch in the Busy Bee Restaurant in the center of town. The clientele are friendly and the food is good. Before coming to the restaurant, we had purchased some maple sugar and maple syrup from a local distributor.

I knew a little about the sugaring process from conversations with my father. I still had some questions. There was a man sitting at the counter of the restaurant as we talked about the sugaring process. I knew that the trees would be tapped in late February or early March as the earliest signs of spring would occur.

I asked the man who appeared to be a Glover native how high the snow would be as he set out to tap his trees. His answer was "Oh, about four feet. We go in on snow shoes." This man appeared to be just shy of six feet tall. He then said "I have to reach up, sometimes, to get the pail when I return for the sap."

As I stood looking over the farmland, I could imagine my great grandfather, Joseph, going out to close a gate or tend to a distressed animal with a blizzard blowing across that wide expanse in sub zero temperatures. My urban, southern New England life suddenly seemed more comfortable.

Sugaring has been a constant over the 200 plus years of Glover's existence. For a period of time in history, the tending of sheep was an important activity as well. Beginning in the 1830s, the tending of Merino sheep was an important activity. The textile mills of Manchester, New Hampshire, and farther south in Lowell, Massachusetts, caused the price of wool to be high. Merino wool was in demand.[29]

The numbers of sheep on Vermont farms increased between 1810 and 1840 from 22, 432 to 1,681,819. In 1840 Glover had 4, 797 sheep.[30] I don't have statistics for the number of sheep on Joseph's farm for this era. He did not have any sheep in 1870. After the Civil War, sheep breeders headed west. It would be easy to imagine sheep grazing on the pastures near the top of Sheffield Heights.

Actually, Albert had twelve sheep on his farm in 1870.[31] The hilly pastures now suited for the Belgian horses on the Johnson farm today would also be suitable for Albert's sheep of 1870 or a larger flock during the Merino sheep heyday. The loss of income from the wool sales may have had its effect as Glover's population declined after the Civil War.

As the 1860s began, the needs of the Civil War emerged. Unlike the War of 1812 when Vermonters felt that this was not their war, the Civil War was a cause that they felt deserved support. Vermont had outlawed slavery since its inception as a state.[32] The western part of the state at St. Albans was the last step on the Underground Railway.[33]

This "railway" was a system that allowed black slaves to be smuggled from their owners in the southern states through a series of stops going north toward Canada as the final destination. Vermont had a stake in the freedom of slaves.

Many men of Glover contributed to the formation of the Vermont Brigade that had an impressive battle record. One of these men was Carlos W. Dwinell.

Carlos Dwinell rose to the rank of Major. Unfortunately, he died of wounds received at the Battle of Charleston, Virginia, on August 24, 1864.

Very little is said of Carlos except by Maria Hemenway.[34] His impressive military record is engraved on his marker in the cemetery at the junction of Routes 16 and 122 in Glover. Carlos is a rather distant relative of mine. Actually, Carlos is the great, great grandson of my great, great, great, great, great grand uncle. We share the same person as the first known Dwinell in America as a relative. His military record is mentioned here to indicate that the young men of Glover responded. Carlos saw action in many of the fiercest battles of the war, including Gettysburg and Antietam.

In 1874 Joseph's son, Dwight, received an undivided half of the family farm for the price of $2,000. Dwight is my grandfather. Specifically, the farm consisted of 60 acres from Lots 83, 40 acres from Lot 86, the north part of Lot 84, one acre from Lot 85 and 20 acres from Lot 61.[35] The specifics of this transaction recorded here will aid in the clarity of future land deals in the Dwinell family, particularly as it relates to my father.

In a map of Glover developed in the 1870s the farm is in the area of Sheffield Heights with acreage of 160 acres. It is marked on the map as belonging to J. Dwinell and D. J. Dwinell. Solomon Dwinell had a farm of 80 acres on Lot 81 or 82. Albert Dwinell had retained his 80-acre farm on Lot 63. At this point in history, Solomon, his sons and his grandson had 320 acres of farmland in Glover.

The population of Glover had peaked at 1,250 in 1860. In 1880 it would be 1,070.[36]Part of this population decline would be due to smaller families. Part of the decline would be due to the migration. By 1900 the Glover population would be 900. The United States was making progress. Other opportunities presented themselves.

Joseph's son, Dwight, soon sold the farm. The sale was back to Joseph. This sale would have an effect on my father later in the century. The sale would have broken the tradition of sales of land to one's son to preserve the family legacy. My father was only a teenager at the time.

Dwight had begun a carpenter's business in Glover. He had talent as a carpenter and cabinet-maker. It was later proved that he had talent as a sculptor as well. Joseph remained on the farm until his death in 1899. His son, Dwight, had left Glover in 1891 for St. Johnsbury, Vermont, to pursue his skill as a carpenter and to send his children to school.[37]

My father, Rolland D. Dwinell, received part of the farm as the result of a note arrangement with his grandmother. She was Ann Cook Dwinell, Joseph's wife. The farm was then sold back to Rolland's grandmother on a subsequent note arrangement. It appears that Rolland received part of the farm from his father, Dwight, and, then, managed the total farm for his grandmother. Rolland was only fifteen when Dwight went to St. Johnsbury, so it may have been necessary to create a different land conveyance arrangement to deed the farm to Rolland when he became of age. There is more detail to this arrangement that will emerge as we discuss the life of Rolland Dwinell..

The oldest Dwinell photograph of which I am aware is of Joseph Dwinell. My sister, Margaret, has this photograph. He is a severe looking chap. It is not difficult for me to believe that he was a farmer in the rugged environment of the Northeast Kingdom. He appears to have husbanded the legacy of this farmland well. The census of 1870 demonstrates an impressive enterprise.

Solomon Dwinell began the Vermont legacy with an investment of $270 for 80 acres in 1817. This investment turned into 320 acres for himself and his sons several decades later. It took hard work and a family effort.

No wonder the Vermont heritage is laconic and independent. Imagine Solomon, Joseph or Albert alone on the hill of their respective farm with inclement weather and the need to complete a task before they head for shelter. By inclement weather I mean a balmy forty degrees below zero Fahrenheit with thirty or forty miles per hour winds or a blizzard with temperatures nearly as low.

What was their shelter like before central heating or indoor plumbing? How did they get through a winter in this small town? Roughly, the population of Glover at its height was one person for each 18 acres of land. One's neighbors were not nearby.

There is a turning point as we look at the life of my grandfather, Dwight Joseph Dwinell. Remember, as we look at his decisions that he grew up on a farm and helped run it for awhile. Life goes on for all the participants in a family.

As my grandfather, Dwight, was making a career decision, his parents were still running the family farm. Dwight's children were older now and were soon to face a life ultimately of their choice. Also, property was still in existence and the decisions regarding this property were in flux. We need to finish business in Glover before we return to St. Johnsbury and Dwight.

Dwight's sons and his daughter had farm life as their legacy as well. The people we will meet in the emergent generation are not far removed from the rugged life of the Northeast Kingdom.

Joseph Dwinell, Dwight's father, is the only player in this drama who is totally a product of the Northeast Kingdom of Vermont farm life. He was born, lived and died a farmer. He was a success.

Joseph died at age 77 after a fruitful life in a rugged setting.[38] As he turned his farm over to his wife and his 23-year old grandson, he must have wondered what was in store for them. There are two stories about to emerge. The decision of my grandfather to go to St. Johnsbury is the first story. Then, we will explore how this decision had an effect on my father, Rolland, in both the short and the long run. He was Joseph's 23 year old grandson who was to continue the agricultural legacy. We can return, now, to St. Johnsbury and the life of my grandfather and grandmother and their children.

My grandfather, Dwight Joseph Dwinell, was born at the family farm on May 27, 1851.[39] He grew up in this farm environment and worked the farm until he was forty years old. On October 21, 1856, Dwight married Julia L. Merriam in Glover, Vermont.[40] The Merriam family had a substantial farm that abutted the southwestern edge of the Dwinell farm. Julia's father, William Merriam, was a well-known figure in farm circles in the community of Glover.[41]

While exploring the reference section of the Littleton, New Hampshire, library, I ran across the obituary notice in a St. Johnsbury, Vermont, paper[42] for my grandmother, Julia Dwinell. The obituary notice stated that Dwight and Julia had come to the city from their Glover farm, because they wanted their children to be educated. The children of Dwight and Julia, Rolland, Carl, Dean and Clara, were successful. Dwight's grandchildren all had college degrees. Dwight and Julia deserve a great deal of credit for realizing in 1891 that this provision for their children's education was important. With the passing of his wife, my grandfather was alone, now, as he thought of his children. He had a right to be proud of his decision.

Dwight and Julia had four children, Rolland, Carl, Dean and Clara.[43] Each would become uniquely successful in careers other than farming as they matured. Clara became a teacher in Orleans and Barton, Vermont. Dean became a retailer and a manufacturer as well as a representative to the Vermont Legislature. Carl became a building contractor, and my father, Rolland, became a factory foreman.

Dwight remained in St. Johnsbury as a carpenter and contractor until 1897. He then moved to the capital city of Montpelier, Vermont. He started working in the Sergeant of Arms office if the State House in 1902. He was appointed deputy in 1913 and became the head of the department as Sergeant of Arms in 1917. He built a home on Dwinell Street in 1904, so he became well established in the neighborhood. Dwinell Street is named for Dwight.[44]

The role of Sergeant at Arms is part ceremonial and part functional. Essentially, Dwight was the superintendent of the Capitol Building and grounds. He would also perform ceremonial functions as special sessions would be held at the

State House. He worked as the Sergeant at Arms for 23 years. In this role, he became a well-known figure in Montpelier.

There is a family story that speaks to the reputation that Dwight enjoyed. When my wife, Ann, obtained her first teaching job, we decided to celebrate by taking a trip to New Hampshire. We invited my sister, Margaret, along. Margaret soon became the tour guide as we decided to visit Vermont as well. Our children always looked to Margaret as someone who was fun loving and somewhat more permissive than their parents. Soon after we started on our trip from Littleton, New Hampshire, we stopped for lunch at a small restaurant just across the border into Vermont. We were to wend our way south to Montpelier after lunch.

After we had sandwiches, one of the children suggested dessert. Ann and I were ready to oblige. The otherwise permissive Aunt Margaret had other ideas as she said, "Did you come here to sight see or to eat?" We were all surprised, so the dessert was scratched. When it comes to Vermont, Aunt Margaret can be very serious. When we arrived at the street in front of the Vermont State House, there was a tour-guide booth on the sidewalk with a very pleasant woman in charge. I suggested to Theresa, our oldest child, that she should sign the guest book. When the tour guide saw the name, *Dwinell* she became quite effusive.

She immediately turned her duties over to another person to give us a private tour. As we walked toward the State House, she spoke of my grandfather, the great grandfather of Theresa and our other children. When we arrived at the main floor entrance, there was an office to the left. On the wall adjacent to the office was a rather large picture of Dwight. Our children, particularly Theresa, had seen this picture before. Theresa was impressed; maybe the boys were as well.

The tour guide told us a story as she walked along that is well known in Montpelier. There is a wood carving of Ceres atop the State House dome. The people of Vermont refer to the statue as the Goddess of Agriculture. Ann knew Ceres as the goddess of fertility. This revelation reinforced Ann's view that we Dwinells were adequately prolific.

There is more to the story of this carving. When Dwight was 87 years old, he superintended the project of creating the Ceres statue. He did much of the carving himself. Our daughter, Theresa, has a picture of Dwight at work on the statue. The project was budgeted for an amount that Dwight felt was too expensive. He announced that he would do the job himself.[45]

Dwight was selected eleven times for the position of Sergeant at Arms. When he passed away at age 89, his son, Carl, assumed the role. Carl was a successful contractor in Vermont.[46]

Dwight gave us a different direction and was the first Dwinell to appear to have an artistic flair. His youngest child, Clara, would become a teacher in Orleans and Barton, Vermont. His youngest son, Dean, became a retailer and then a manufacturer of clothing. His son, Carl, was a successful contractor. Ultimately, his oldest son, Rolland, became a factory foreman of a small church-pew production company. Essentially, he was the production manager of this company.

The records of the St. Johnsbury Academy were destroyed by fire after Dwight's children may have attended this school. Family tradition suggests that they did attend and, perhaps, some of them graduated. I know that Carl had attended, since he responded to an alumni request stating that he was there for a short time.[47] My father used to receive newsletters from the school.

The suggestion was there, though. Education was an item to be discussed. As the ninth generation emerged, the impetus started by Dwight as he left the farm in Glover became a new direction for the family.

My father, Rolland Dwinell, was the oldest son. Traditionally, the responsibility and opportunity of ownership went to the first son. However, Rolland's father had left farm life behind. This fact created a problem that Joseph, his wife, Ann, and ultimately, Rolland would face.

The fact that my father had the resources to resolve this problem eventually indicates that Dwight had provided direction that allowed Rolland to grow as he took advantage of the opportunities before him and coped with the problems they presented.

My father was born on March 29, 1876. The 1880 Census shows that Dwight, Julia, their daughter, Clara, and their two oldest sons, Rolland and Carl, lived on the family farm owned by Joseph and Dwight Dwinell.[48]

Rolland grew up on the family farm until he was fourteen or fifteen in 1891. It is unclear what happened to the boys when Julia and Dwight went to St. Johnsbury. My cousin, Alice, has indicated that Dwight and Julia's daughter, Clara, went to live with her Aunt Irene Nye in Orleans. Irene Nye was Dwight's sister.

Given Dwight's statement in the newspaper account of why he went to St. Johnsbury, it seems that the parents' intent was that the boys attend St. Johnsbury Academy. There are some factors that indicate that my father may have been at the Academy for some time. He may well have graduated.

He appeared to know abstract mathematics reasonably well. I can remember how he helped Margaret and Clara. It appears to me that he played the Sousaphone in the Academy band. The subject came up several times in our family.

There are two pictures of him in uniform as part of the Glover Coronet Band. In each case, he is holding what appears to be a Sousaphone rather than a coronet.[49] If he did attend St. Johnsbury Academy until graduation, he would have been ready for the real world about 1895 or 1896. Perhaps, he returned to the farm at about age 18 to 20.

I have heard family stories about his life as a lumberjack. As a farmer, he would have the time to be a lumberjack during the winter. My father was very thin until he reached his sixties. One story I have heard is that he was a topper. This was a job for a light, agile person. The topper would climb to near the top of the tree in order to cut off the unwanted top. He had to be careful. If his cut did not go all the way through, he could have been "spread eagled" with each leg on two rapidly splitting portions of the tree. As an 18–20 year old young man, he could have played that role.

There is another story. He was a lumberjack foreman. One winter he went into the woods with his crew to work through the winter. In March he and the crew came out of the woods to a nearby town. In those days, quite often the best place to eat was the local bar. My father did not drink. He decided to go to the bank for the payroll to compensate his men then to the local barbershop for a bath, haircut and shave. They had been in the woods all winter. Their beards were full, and they were quite unkempt.

After his trip to the barber shop, it was time to pay his men. Also, he was hungry, so he went to the bar where his men were drinking and, hopefully, eating. As he entered the bar, he approached them to pay them for a winter's work. They didn't recognize him. He had a hard time convincing them to accept their pay.

I don't know where he worked on this lumbering job. There was a person in the Glover area who bought timber from farmers including Rolland.[50] He had a large operation in the Bridgton, Maine area. I've heard stories of the huge birch trees in northern New Hampshire that he cut. There are other possibilities. It would seem this activity took place between 1895 and 1900. As we shall see later, it may also have taken place after 1911.

In 1893, Rolland's mother died. His father stayed in St. Johnsbury until 1897. Then, it appears that the boys were on their own to seek their own destiny. Dean found his way to Lebanon, New Hampshire, then back to Newport, Vermont. Carl appears to have stayed in Glover as a teacher in the West Glover Graded School. His daughter, my cousin Alice, tells me that he taught the entire non-graded school. Carl eventually moved to Orleans to start his contracting business. It appears that my father divided his time between the farm and his lumberjack role.

Rolland married Eva Baldic on June 25, 1900, in Glover. Unfortunately, she died on March 12, 1901.[51] Rolland's grandfather had died in 1899, so he and Eva had been living on the family farm with his grandmother, Ann Cook Dwinell, during this time. Rolland married Sarah Johnson on October 9, 1902.[52] They continued living on the family farm. About a year after their marriage, they would lose their prematurely born son.

When Rolland's grandfather died in 1899, he received an undivided half interest in the farm in satisfaction of a note that appeared as a credit against the estate.[53] He appeared eventually to have managed the entire farm for his grandmother.

As of now, I am not aware of the origin of the note. When Dwight relinquished the farm back to Joseph back in 1891, Rolland was a minor. This note may have been part of that transaction. This action would preserve the tradition of the transfer of land to the oldest son, first.

There is a series of complex transactions regarding Lots 61, 83, 84, 85, and 86 that show that Rolland owned the farm with his grandmother and wife, Sarah, until April 11, 1909, when Rolland's grandmother died.[54] Then in 1911, something happened. Evidently, Rolland's grandmother died intestate requiring a distribution following statutory law.

The distribution of Ann Dwinell's estate appears to have gone to Dwight Dwinell and Dwight's sister, Irene Nye. Rolland did not receive the land he had anticipated receiving. Just before the death of Ann Proctor Dwinell, Joseph's wife, and immediately there after, there was a series of real estate transactions involving the family's estate. Rolland returned his half share in the farm to the estate of Ann Dwinell in satisfaction of the note against the deeded right to one half interest in the farm received at the time of the death of his grandfather in 1899.

The farm in its entirety was distributed to Dwight Dwinell, Rolland's father, and Irene Nye, Rolland's aunt. Rolland and his wife, Sarah, did own 20 acres of the southwest portion of Lot 60. This farm land was nearly two full lots south of lots 83 and 84 at the peak of Sheffield Heights. This property was almost a mile due south downhill from the family farm.

Sarah and Rolland would live in Glover until Sarah's death. During this time Rolland appears to have worked as a lumber jack to supplement his lesser level of income on this smaller farm

It does appear that Sarah and Rolland must have struggled. Rolland appears to have left the farm to become a lumberjack. His wife Sarah died on August 24,

1914.[55] She was 53 years old. After Sarah's death, Rolland made a career decision.

My sister, Margaret, tells me that in 1915 Rolland came to Lowell, Massachusetts, from Sheffield, Vermont, with "Aunt Belle." Aunt Belle appears to be the aunt of my cousins, Alice and Dwight Dwinell. Her name is Belle Cameron. They made the trek in a Model T Ford. This journey could not have been easy. There is a picture in the "History of the town of Glover, Vermont" with the caption "Helping Out—circa 1923." It shows a cart with a team of oxen getting an automobile out of a rut. It was not easy to drive in 1923, or 1915.

What would it have been like to drive through Franconia Notch? Lowell is a city of 90 to 100,000 people. Pictures of Lowell in this era show cobble-stoned streets in the downtown area. The pictures on the edge of the city show dirt roads. The roads from northern Vermont to northern Massachusetts would have presented a challenge. It appears that Rolland came to Lowell at about this time to start life alone.

My mother has told me that my father experienced abject poverty and worked as a railway express person. I know that he returned to Sheffield, Vermont, in 1917 to sell his lumbering tools for $100. His life in Vermont was now behind him.

His draft registration application for World War I shows that he was gainfully employed in Lowell.[56] The application indicates that Rolland was a lumber surveyor for the Burnham-Davis Company, a Lowell lumber business. He was living then at 97 Grand Street, quite close to downtown Lowell.

He met my mother, Theresa Scullen, in Lowell and they were married on September 2, 1919.[57] Theresa had recently emigrated from the town of Toombridge in Northern Ireland. She had worked in a linen mill in Moneymore in Northern Ireland before coming to America. When she first arrived in this country, she was employed in Lowell at the Merrimack Mills. Her sponsors when she came to Lowell were the O'Neill family who lived on Lombard Street in the heart of what was then called Lowell's Irish Acre.

Their Marriage License Application indicates that she was a waitress who was living at 38 Branch Street in Lowell. Rolland was living at that time at 93 Westford Street where my sisters and I were born.

Rolland and Theresa would lose two children in childbirth before we were born. Then, my father's fortunes changed. He had a very difficult life from the time his mother died in 1893 until he married and started a family with Theresa. He was a very frugal, careful man. Given his experiences, this frugality is understandable even beyond his Yankee disposition.

Soon after his work at Burnham-Davis, he became the foreman of the Amasa Pratt Company at the western end of Dutton Street in Lowell. The company manufactured church pews. His job was to supervise cabinet-makers and stainers as well as being the purchasing agent of lumber and supplies and, essentially, the production manager and chief operating officer.

My father would see his brother, Carl, quite often. We would go to Orleans or Carl and his family would come to Lowell. When the adults had a chance to talk, invariably, an argument would break out between Carl and Rolland.

Carl was a small business owner. My father was a foreman hiring men who had to support their families. As the Depression deepened and continued seemingly endlessly, President Roosevelt instituted many liberal programs designed to put money in the pockets of the unemployed.[58] My father had converted to Roosevelt's ideas but not my uncle. These programs presented a short-term cost for the small business owner.

More than 119 years prior Thomas Malthus had said that expenditures by consumers would be needed to support an economy with an increasing population. Most economic observers rejected his theories. Roosevelt was trying to get the American consumer to be able to consume again. A British economist named John Maynard Keynes was saying the same thing that Malthus had said but with a more incisive body of theory. The argument raged not only between my father and my uncle—it raged across the land. Today, we have a similar argument in our society.

On those walks that I would take to downtown Lowell, I would drop in to see my father at his factory. The men knew me well and were always pleasant to me. He would be operating one of two saws. One saw was the crosscut saw that would cut the lumber to the desired length. The other saw was the ripsaw that would cut the wood to the desired width. There was always a huge pile of lumber to be placed into production. First, he had to make those exact cuts.

Next door was the Parker Company that made industrial wooden bobbins for the textile industry. Their industrial wood lathes would shave the wood to the precise size. As a result, there was always a huge pile of sawdust out the open door of my father's factory.

I always had a vague sense of unease when I saw that saw dust. I didn't know why. In the summer without air conditioning I could smell the saw dust aroma. I know, now, that there was the danger of spontaneous combustion. I am glad that I didn't know why then. I'm sure that my father was aware of the danger.

I remember that he worked Monday through Friday and usually went in on Saturday morning, even during the Depression. He had an active life at home as well.

When we first lived on Sayles Street, he has said that he needed to use two kegs of nails to better secure the clapboards on the house. He had a vegetable garden that was quite productive.

His hobby was short-wave radio. As a result, he installed an aerial system among three houses in the neighborhood to give him and two of his neighbors better reception. In 1936 be bought a short-wave radio for $300. It allowed him to listen to ham radio operators and radio stations across the United States and in Europe. My father would listen to baseball games from Brooklyn and New York as well as Boston.

I can remember his listening to Adolph Hitler from Munich and Berlin. As far as I know, my father did not know German. He could tell though that something was unique about Hitler, even in the 1936 era. He would tell us that this was a dangerous man.

He would record the call letters of ham radio operators, score baseball and football games and read the paper from cover to cover—two or three more papers when Clara and I had the paper route. He wanted to compile and absorb whatever he got his hands on. He had a keen interest in the progress of World War II. As he sat at home recovering from frequent coronary attacks, he would absorb as much as he could from radio and the newspapers.

His interest in radio was long standing. A family artifact was a small table in our parents' bedroom. This table had a crude arrangement of a set of wires and devices. I learned that this was a crystal set that served in the 1920s as a home-made radio. The best way to describe this device is to have you imagine a very smart fourth grade student who took on the project of creating a radio as a science project.

We all enjoyed this new, more modern radio, then. On Monday nights at 9:00 p.m. we would listen to the "Lux Radio Theatre" with Cecil D. DeMille. We would hear "The Shadow" at 4:30 p.m. on Saturday. Friday night at 7:30 was "Grand Central Station." We heard Jack Benny, "Fibber Magee and Molly" and "The Lone Ranger"—the list goes on.

Rolland worked at Amasa Pratt until the early 1940s. When the company began to have financial difficulties, he could have retired. However, we were at war, and he felt that he should do his part. He took a job at the Quincy Naval Shipyard and commuted daily. This era was before Route 128 and the Southeast

Expressway. There were no Interstate Highways then. It was a long ride on what we now refer to as secondary highways.

When he began to have coronary trouble, my mother felt that it was that long commute. We lived about a mile and a half from the Pratt Company and he was the boss. This was a different situation. He died of a heart attack on July 13, 1947. He was 71 years old.

Beyond his Yankee frugality, there were other telltale signs that he was a Vermonter. He would tell us that you could always tell a good farmer, because his barn would look better than his house. He would pronounce the word cow as caow as though there were a diphthong sound. Also, my Uncle Carl would send him a gallon of Vermont maple syrup every year at Christmas. My father would have a cereal bowl full of the syrup each night before bed.

He was the last vestige of our family tie to agriculture. He came to Lowell to a different economy, a more technical environment and a faster paced society, Although he didn't want Margaret, and perhaps Clara, to go to college, he set knowledge as a goal for us. Sometimes the role model you present is more effective than the words you use. Ordinarily, he was a man of a few words, but you knew what he meant.

The turning point of our family's experience came when Dwight decided to move to St. Johnsbury so his children could have an education. Our family should feel grateful to him for showing us the way, but my father paid a short run price. The hardship endured as the result of the loss of the farm had its advantage, though. He had the drive to succeed in a new environment. The example he set caused his children to succeed.

We have a heritage of accomplishment and independence. To a large degree these traits come from our Vermont legacy. This heritage is an extension of the farm legacy that originally came from Michael Dwinell, Sr., and was passed down through the generations.

He was a proud man. Rolland was an excellent example of teaching by example. He taught me to be value free as he accepted people as he found them. This is the Dwinell heritage I know. This heritage is apparent in the lives of the men who came before Rolland.

6

The Emergent Generation

"There comes a time in every man's education, when he arrives at the conviction that envy is ignorance; that imitation is suicide; that he must take himself for better for worse as his portion...."

—*Ralph Waldo Emerson in "Self Reliance"*

I always feel at home as I travel in New Hampshire or Vermont. Even when I am sure that I have never been in a specific location before, I feel that I know where I am. Part of this feeling comes from those sojourns from Lowell, Massachusetts, to Montpelier or Orleans, Vermont, in a 1938 Plymouth. I am told that we used to make these treks in a Model T Ford, but I don't remember those experiences.

The 1938 Plymouth would be an improvement on the Model T Ford. It seemed so large even when I was crowded in between my two sisters in the back seat. The trips were interesting when we finally reached the mountains. The trips to Vermont were interesting as well. It seemed that we were entering a different country.

My mother, two sisters and I would crowd in as passengers with my father acting as driver, navigator, storyteller and the otherwise quiet patriarch of the Dwinell family. My mother would keep me distracted, so I wouldn't react to the motion of the car. Picture my father as the typical Northeast Kingdom of Vermont farmer and my mother as the typical Irish mother of our active family.

The other part of this feeling of familiarity with New Hampshire and Vermont has a mystical quality that I hope this book explains, at least to me. I relive this mysticism frequently.

Quite coincidentally, my wife, Ann, and I own property at Lake Winnipesaukee just down the hill in Meredith, New Hampshire, from the point on Route 3 that provided me with the first view of the mountains. These particular mountains in the foreground due north are the Sandwich Mountains, the foothills of the White Mountains farther north.

These mountains seemed so close. We would picnic near Lake Squam. Then, about two hours later we would be in Franconia Notch. I didn't know why it took us so long to get to those mountains. I understand, now.

The oldest Dwinell within my memory span is my grandfather. He was a rather short but stately gentleman who had an aura of importance about him. I don't remember, though, that he was a self-centered person. My eldest cousin, Lane, could be described the same way. They had good cause for this aura they possessed as well as the confidence to avoid self-import. I discern, though, that there is self-assurance among the Dwinell family members who I know. This self-confidence should not be elevated to a sense of aura, but the assurance is there.

Recently, the events of the late 1930s regarding my rides to Montpelier to visit grandfather and to Orleans to visit our uncle and his family were revisited. My two sisters, Margaret and Clara, and our cousin, Alice, rode from Medford, Massachusetts, to Lebanon, New Hampshire. We were going to the funeral of our cousin, Lane Dwinell. Although the road was on a direct series of Interstate Highways, I could remember the old Routes 3 and 4, the superhighways of the thirties and forties. The terrain was similar although both the car and highways were larger.

The Lebanon Congregational Church has the same simple but impressive design of so many other New England churches. Its cemetery is simple as well. Lane had been the governor of New Hampshire and had held several important federal roles as the eulogies offered at the funeral ceremony indicated. Yet, in keeping with the true Yankee spirit, the surroundings and the simple DWINELL on the headstone in the cemetery behind the church spoke volumes. The spring mud and the beginning of a substantial snowstorm added to the stark environment. This snowstorm has come to be known as the April Fools Day Storm of 1997, since it began on March 31 and continued into the next day.

My daughter, Theresa, and her older son, Vincent, joined us at the ceremony. They, too, had driven to Lebanon from farther south. Theresa was living in Londonderry, New Hampshire at the time. The two eulogies presented Lane's life appropriately.

The former governor of New Hampshire, John Sununu, recounted Lane's political career. The governor knew Lane well professionally and was able to recount Lane's impressive career. The other speaker was a man named John Newman. John is the nephew of Lane and knew Lane as an uncle who had done much to help John as a person. John is the son of Lane's sister, Eleanor Dwinell Newman Borella. Unfortunately, Eleanor's marriage to Albert Newman had ended in divorce when John Newman was only five years' old. John's eulogy fittingly was about how much Lane's contribution was appreciated as Lane provided a male presence for John. As I have learned about John's life, I have understood his remarks better.

Lane and his wife, Elizabeth Cushman Dwinell, would have been good parents. I didn't know his wife, Betty as she was known in the family, very well. Despite his impressive political stature, I knew Lane as a very thoughtful and outgoing person who always had time for family and a continued discussion of the Dwinell legacy. To a large degree, he started me on this attempt to chronicle the family. Lane was interested in anyone named Dwinell. I am interested in a chronicle in some depth of our direct line of descent. Lane, though, knew a great deal about our heritage as is evidenced by his memberships as a Son of the American Revolution and a Descendant of the Colonial Wars.

Seymour Lane Dwinell was born in Newport, Vermont, to Ruth and Dean Dwinell. Seymour Lane is the name of Ruth Dwinell's father, so Lane was named for his maternal grandfather. He soon became known as Lane. Lane's date of birth is November 14, 1904.[1] Newport, Vermont, is the County Seat of Orleans County. Newport also serves as a rail gateway to Canada on Vermont's northern border. It is one of two important cities in the fabled Northeast Kingdom of Vermont. While Newport sits at the northwest corner of this region, St. Johnsbury lies at the southeast corner of the Kingdom. As the result of Newport's regional importance, Lane was able to lead an active and interesting childhood in Newport.

An early record of Lane's experience is depicted in a newspaper photograph of his fourth grade class in the Graded School of Newport, Vermont, in 1914. His classmates included several people who would become important. These people included Victor Borella who became the executive-vice-president of Rockefeller Center in New York City as well as an aide to Governor Nelson Rockefeller, Henry F. Black who became an attorney and a Superior Court Judge and Winston Prouty who became the United States Senator from Vermont.[2] Lane's father, my uncle Dean, ran a shoe store in Newport and had been a representative from Newport to the Vermont Legislature. He also had been a member of the Newport City Council. Particularly as a teenager, Lane had an active life in Newport due mainly to his father's business contacts.

I had the good fortune to acquire the personal diary of Lane that covered the years from 1922 to 1926. These years began with the second half of his sophomore year in high school. The diary continued until the first half of his junior year in college. The entries depicted a very involved and thoughtful young man who accepted life positively and exercised a very conscientious and sustained effort in every task and involvement he encountered.

His high school career was spent in Newport, Vermont, Pasadena, California, and Lebanon, New Hampshire. In each of these schools Lane was able to excel both as a student and an athlete. He also found time to be a very conscientious member of the Congregational Church at each of these locations. His athletic interests included basketball, baseball, track, football and snow shoeing.

His scholastic achievements were in rigorous subject matter, particularly foreign languages. He found time to be active in stage performances even acting as a minstrel show interlocutor. This era was the age of Vaudeville. Part of the Vaudeville era was the emergence of the Minstrel Show.

Like Vaudeville, the Minstrel Show combined familiar popular music with comic acts to provide a unique brand of entertainment. Minstrel Show performers entertained in Black Face, since the new Jazz Age musical medium originated with black people from the south. The humor tried to mimic the humor of the Southern Black of the United States.

Eventually, the Black community reacted. These people felt that they were diminished and exploited by this type of entertainment. Soon, the minstrel shows faded. For a time through the twenties, thirties and into the forties it was a form of entertainment for both professional and amateur.

As Lane assumed the role of the interlocutor, he would have had to assume a clever comic role. He would have been the lead comic as well as the emcee of the musical show.

As a result of this stage experience, he became interested in speech organizations. His ability to adapt to changing environments and his affinity to people is exemplified by his election to the office of secretary to the senior class of Lebanon High School. He had just moved to Lebanon after his junior year at Newport High School in Vermont.

As all of this was happening, Lane maintained a strong family life. He worked hard every summer in Newport doing physical work, particularly the painting of buildings in downtown Newport. Later, he would work in the family factory and store in Lebanon. When the family moved to Lebanon, Lane's father, Dean Dwinell, opened a new shoe store and also became a partner in the Carter Churchill Company. This company manufactured a line of outdoor clothing.

Lane's college career at Dartmouth College was spent in the same rigorous pursuit of the liberal arts. He continued his athletic interests at Dartmouth in track and snow shoeing. He also pursued an interest in ski jumping. In addition to all this, Lane was an avid golfer. Lane is the first intercollegiate athlete I have found in our direct line of descent.

As I read his diary, it appeared that the active social life he led pursued a younger version of the adult life of the fabled Roaring Twenties. The American Spirit after a war that for many was a disillusioning experience chose the period of the 1920s to spread its collective wings.

Lane's father's business interests took him to Pasadena, California, for Lane's sophomore year in high school. Lane appears to have adapted to Southern California well—both academically and socially. Although he was a rather conservative, god-fearing young man from northern New England, Lane enjoyed Southern California. Access to the family car gave him a social lift as he enjoyed high school life in Pasadena.

There is one set of entries in his diary about his trip home to Vermont and its immediate aftermath. Just before the family left on the California Limited to return home by train, his father placed the family car on a transport ship for its return to the East Coast.

When the family returned home in June, it was some time into mid July before the car arrived at the port of Boston. Lane was quite anxious regarding the car. Even in 1922, the lack of a car was cramping this sixteen-year-old young man's style.

He was a serious young man, though. As early as June, 1922, at the end of his sophomore year in high school, he had decided to become a lawyer. This decision would explain his pursuit of the liberal arts. His subsequent career as a businessman and a politician would explain his interest in the law.

Lane appeared to make the transition from high school to college easily. He was a good student in high school as a member of the National Honor Society. In his senior year, he pursued other interests as well and expanded his athletic, social and extra curricular horizons.

He continued to work hard at Dartmouth. He lived at college and appears to have adapted well to dormitory life. He studied hard, became involved in campus life and continued to pursue his athletic interests. He always had time for his religion, and as his sister was approaching mid adolescence, he always made time for her.

There are many references in his diary to his communications with "Elly", the family name for Eleanor. He would write to her, telephone her from his room and take her to the movies quite frequently. His parents traveled a good deal, but Eleanor's big brother was there for her.

This young man appeared to have an eager love for life. He accomplished a great deal, but he apparently had his feet on the ground and accepted people as he found them. This is the Lane Dwinell who I knew.

I'm sure that I had met him many times when I was a boy. Some of those sojourns to Montpelier to see grandfather involved a stopover at Lebanon. My first real memory of Lane, though, was at my Uncle Carl's funeral in 1950. My mother and I borrowed my sister, Clara's, relatively new car to attend the funeral services in Orleans, Vermont. After the services, Lane invited us back to his home in Lebanon, New Hampshire.

I was a twenty-year-old college sophomore with limited driving experience. In fact, the last time I had driven a car, I had had an encounter with a bus at an intersection in Lowell. The bus won. I totaled the family car I was using to transport fellow students from Lowell to college in Salem, Massachusetts.

Lane was in his early forties and had been driving New Hampshire's roads since 1922. As we left Orleans to head south, we passed through several towns on Vermont's Route 5 and comparable New Hampshire routes. This era was before Interstate Highways, so the roads were what we now refer to as secondary roads. Lane kept his car going at fifty miles per hour no matter what was happening around him or where we were. Even then I knew that this was a young man on the move.

Much has been written about Lane's business and political career. I will try to encapsulate that career in the paragraphs to follow. I hope the account of his early years tells us about the person. To me he was that regular guy I knew as my cousin.

Lane graduated from Dartmouth College in 1928. He was the first member of our direct line of descent in the Dwinell family to obtain a degree. He would go on to receive a Master's degree in Commercial Science from the Amos Tuck School of Dartmouth. The Tuck School has a long-standing strong reputation in the field of business administration. The MCS degree is the forerunner of today's MBA.

Before attending the Tuck School, Lane would take a tour of Europe in the summer of 1928. The letters that he sent home to his girl friend and future wife, Elizabeth Cushman, revealed a sophisticated and thoughtful young man who took good advantage of this opportunity. I had received a series of letters from the same source as the diary referred to previously. Lane did well in graduate school as he had at Dartmouth College in his undergraduate years.

He started his business career as a financial analyst for General Motors soon after graduation. He married Elizabeth Cushman in 1932 in Lebanon. They then lived in New York City where Lane was still working for General Motors.[3]

Lane and Betty chose a difficult time to become married. The Great Depression was well underway. The unemployment rate was extremely high and rising, banks were closing and wages were declining for those people fortunate enough to have a job. Life was particularly hard on young people trying to start a career.

In 1932 just before their wedding, Betty received a long letter from a classmate of hers from Emerson College. Her friend had to decline Betty and Lane's invitation to attend their wedding. The letter indicated that this woman and her husband could not afford to come from upstate New York to Lebanon.

The letter described the problems facing this young couple. The husband had just received two successive 10% cuts in pay. Although the landlord had cut the rent recently, this couple and other residents of the apartment complex where they resided needed the rent cut again.

The woman could not find work even though she recently earned her degree. Women were not being hired despite their qualifications—especially with a working husband. Her parents couldn't help. The bank that held their checking account and savings had failed. The economy was low and destined to get worse. Lane and Betty were fortunate. Lane had a job, and they were ready to start life in these troubled times.

In 1935 Lane and Betty returned to Lebanon as Lane became a partner in the Carter Churchill Company. Lane's mother was not well and his father needed help. Dean Dwinell was the principal owner of Carter Churchill. Later Lane would become the principal owner of the company as well as a director of the Lebanon National Bank.

Lane's political career began in 1948 as a member of the New Hampshire Constitutional Convention. He later became a member of the New Hampshire House of Representatives. In 1951, he became the Speaker of the New Hampshire House of Representatives for the 1951–52 legislative session. In the 1952–53 legislative session, Lane became the President of the New Hampshire Senate. In 1954 he became the Governor of New Hampshire. Lane is the first person in the history of the state to become the Speaker of the House, President of the Senate and Governor of the state in successive Legislative Sessions. He served New Hampshire for two terms as its governor.[4]

These were interesting times to be a legislator and then a governor. World War II had ended, but the Korean War was waging. There was a continuing military and political threat of communism. Americans lived with the constant threat of a nuclear attack.

President Eisenhower was able to use the Communist threat to institute an Interstate Highway System for the nation. This improved highway system was designed to be an effective evacuation route in the event of impending nuclear attack. This scheme was implemented because of favorable federal support for state plans that met the national direction. Governor Dwinell was able to contribute to President Eisenhower's national plan.

Lane, as governor, was able to improve the highways of New Hampshire using this Interstate Highway legislation. He also was able to improve education and make the government more fiscally sound. Though quite conservative in his views, he made considerable social progress during his terms of office.

There was a good deal of social turmoil at this point in our history. A senator from Wisconsin named Joseph McCarthy used the existence of the threat of international communism to further his own political agenda. Senator McCarthy was a self-appointed champion of the cause of anti communism. He was ready to attack the concept of communism in any form by going after people he thought were communists or leaning toward communism.

His prime targets were the Hollywood establishment and the United States State Department personnel. There were many people in each of these institutions that had liberal views. For McCarthy, a liberal view was synonymous with communist activity.

His pulpit was a sub committee of the United States Senate in concert with the House un-American Activities Committee. McCarthy was the Chairman of the Permanent Investigations Sub Committee of the Senate Committee on Government Operations. Senator McCarthy received national attention on a grand scale as he brought well-known people before his committee. These two committees and particularly Senator McCarthy himself set out to purge the nation of the communists and communist sympathizers.[5]

Twenty years earlier at the lowest point of the Great Depression, there were many groups of people with quite liberal sometimes radical ideas advocated to solve the problems of dramatically high unemployment and the resultant abject poverty.

Also, there was a communist movement in the country. Some young people at the time experimented with the notion that certain portions of communist thought would act as a solution to our economic ills. Other people embraced liberal thought that could not reasonably be construed as communism by anyone with even a rudimentary knowledge of the distinction between liberal and communist thought.[6] Many of these people became part of the mainstream of a serious liberal community who would emerge as leaders in the 1950s.

Senator McCarthy did not make a distinction among these various liberal thinkers. He set out to find people who he felt were liberal threats to his conservative views. Then, he proceeded to attempt to discredit them. In many cases he succeeded. Many people were temporarily disgraced. Some people were permanently disgraced and/or disillusioned. The result of this behavior of McCarthy was many ruined careers and a very nervous nation. Ultimately, McCarthy himself was discredited and the nation returned to normal.

Simultaneous with action in Washington an incident occurred in New Hampshire during Lane Dwinell's terms in the Legislature and lasted into his terms as Governor. There was an Assistant Professor at the University of New Hampshire named Paul Sweezy who was investigated by the New Hampshire Attorney General for teaching communist thought.[7] There was a specific statute in New Hampshire as in other states outlawing this practice. Aside from his teaching, Sweezy contributed to several radical journals and, in fact, published a leftist journal of his own.[8]

Professor Sweezy was a prime target for an anti communist attack. His case went to the United States Supreme Court as a classic academic freedom argument. Ultimately, Sweezy emerged as the leading American scholar in Marxist economic thought. He and Joan Robinson of England were to become the best interpreters of the subject in the entire Western World. He had to fight a tough court battle before he won this distinction. Lane's Attorney General, Louis Whyman, had to fight this long battle in the courts. This episode is mentioned here to show the climate of the times.

This communist scare produced an atmosphere of conformity at this point in history. One aspect of this conformity was the Loyalty Oath. It became necessary to take a loyalty oath to swear to uphold the Constitution of the United States for virtually any federal, state or local governmental job. One normally expects to take this oath when entering military service or accepting a sensitive federal job. This practice of extending the practice to any governmental job was beyond the routine generally prevalent.

Americans accepted this apparent necessity at first. Eventually, the loyalty oath became a cynical necessity growing to a nuisance. People began to realize that the loyalty oath requirement had cynical overtones. The loyalty oath requirement diminished as the 1960s approached.

A companion condition existed in the 1950s. People tended to conform to a perceived norm. This conformist norm fed the social conditions that allowed the loyalty oath mentality to survive as long as it did. A novelist named Sloan Wilson captured this conformity in his novel, "The Man in the Gray Flannel Suit".

The hero of this novel reacted to this conformity as he insisted on being his own man. Actually, men did wear gray flannel suits. This garb became the typical interview suit for aspiring young men on the move. Sloan Wilson captured this conformity in his ground-breaking novel. The current fashion statement was not the issue. The willingness of a society to accept the bounds of conformity was the issue. As happens often in our country, the society reacted and returned to normal.

Meanwhile, Lane was fast becoming a national figure as a strong member of the northeast wing of the Republican Party. He held several leadership positions among the governors of the nation and worked hard to obtain financial returns to the states from the federal government. As he was reelected to a second term, he caught the eye of the Eisenhower Administration.

When President Eisenhower was elected for a second term, Lane was invited, in 1959, into his Administration as the Under Secretary of State for Administration. His job was to administer the State Department budget and to manage the many embassies around the world. This post involved some travel, so he and Betty began the world travels that they would continue for much of the rest of their lives.

There is a story that Lane liked to tell about his nomination to this position. He needed to receive the confirmation of the Senate in order to be appointed to this post. Therefore, it was necessary for Lane to appear before the Senate Foreign Relations Committee. The Chairman of this committee was the erudite and powerful William Fullbright of Arkansas.

When Senator Fullbright was ready to ask the nominee questions he said "Governor, I have only one question to ask. When Senator Cotton of New Hampshire spoke to us about you, he had some wonderful things to say. He called you Lane Dwinell pronounced with the short sound of I. Senator Prouty of Vermont seemed to think highly of you as well but he called you Dwinell with the long sound of I used. My question, governor, is which Senator is correct?" Lane's answer was "It depends on whether you come from Vermont or New Hampshire." Actually Lane tended to pronounce the name with a short I, at least in my company. Each time that I would see him he would ask me how I pronounced our name. I think he wanted to retell this story, which he did.

Lane returned to New Hampshire at the end of the Eisenhower Administration in 1961. He continued with the family business and his work at the bank and in the community of Lebanon. His politics continued. Although he was a well-known figure in the liberal wing of the Republican Party, his politics were really quite conservative, as people from northern New Hampshire tend to be. Actually, the state motto "Live free or die" suggests a more Libertarian persuasion. Lane continued as a conservative voice for Republican values.

As a result of Lane's activism, he was asked by President Richard Nixon to join the Nixon Administration as the Director of Foreign Aid. This post involved Lane and Betty in a great deal of travel around the world. At the end of the first term of Nixon's presidency, Lane was ready to return to New Hampshire. President Nixon thanked Lane for his service and asked him to help with Richard Nixon's reelection campaign.

It is well known that New Hampshire retains the privilege of being the first state in the nation to conduct primary elections to nominate a presidential candidate from each of the parties. Lane, therefore, had the distinction of being the first person in the country to place Richard Nixon in nomination for a second term of office.

My wife, Ann, and I visited Lane in his Lebanon home in the late eighties. He very graciously invited us into his den. Understandably, he very proudly showed us his letter of gratitude from President Nixon for starting Nixon on his journey toward reelection.

Ann and I are very strong Kennedy Democrats from Massachusetts. I am convinced that Lane knew my politics that I inherited from my father. Apparently, he knew that both Ann and I would be polite and respect his values. My father's politics were well known in both Lane's father, Dean's, household and in our mutual uncle Carl's household. My two uncles were businessmen trying to improve their business during the depression. They did not appreciate Roosevelt's somewhat socialistic political practices. My father was an advocate for the working man. This bias occurred because of his Vermont and early Lowell experiences and the vicarious experiences of watching the men he hired struggle.

Lane continued in Republican politics as he helped the campaigns of Presidents Reagan and the first George Bush. He also became the Chairman of the Board of the Lebanon National Bank. Lane held many other state and City of Lebanon positions. He has also set up a foundation in his and his wife's name at Dartmouth College. A wing of the Lebanon Public Library bears his name as the result of his support.

Ann and I had another opportunity to visit Lane when he was in his late eighties. He took us to lunch at the Dartmouth Club in Hanover. He enjoyed lunch with two Manhattans before the meal. After lunch he took us on a tour of the Campus without missing a beat. He was still energetic and enthusiastic.

There was a human side to Lane that a family story bears out. In 1992 we had a family reunion at our cottage in Meredith, New Hampshire. Our oldest grandson was two years old. Lane was 85.

There is a tourist train that runs along the western shore of Lake Winnipesaukee every half-hour from early morning to late evening. We have a sliding door at the back of the cottage that looks out on the tracks. As the whistle of the train blew, three-year-old Joe would run toward the door to wave at the engineer and passengers. Eighty-five-year old Lane would be right behind Joe.

When we kidded Lane, he explained that he was very proud that he was responsible for legislation that made it mandatory for each community of New Hampshire to have rail service. Twelve years later as I was doing more family research in Concord, New Hampshire, I discovered that the study of trains was a life-long hobby that Lane enjoyed. He never forgot his life in Newport, the Montreal Express and the railroad roundhouse that fascinated him as a boy.[9]

Lane had other interests. He had a log cabin on an island that he owned on the Canadian side of Lake Memphremegog. He and his cousin Dwight enjoyed this island and the lake. Ann and I decided to visit Lane for the first time when we saw Betty and him in their 32-foot boat on Lake Winnepesaukee. Ann and I were in our sixteen-foot runabout.

When we talked with him, he told us that the name of his boat was the Raleigh. The Raleigh is the boat shown on the flag of New Hampshire. He indicated that he was not going to use the boat any more. Ann and I indicated that we were thinking of getting a new boat. We promised him that we would name our new boat the Raleigh, Jr., all nineteen feet of our new runabout. He gave us the New Hampshire flag from his boat. Everything Lane did had a reason. I hope the lives of the Dwinell members that follow show that his positive and sustained interest is a family trait. When Lane died at age 90, he had not quite lived as long as the Dwinell with the greatest longevity. Michael Dwinell, Jr., lived until he was 91. Dr. Michael Dwinell, as he was called, lived a long and productive life at the end of the seventeenth century and well into the eighteenth century. Lane wanted to reach this goal.

Lane's sister, Eleanor Dwinell Newman Borella, was born on February 15, 1911, in Newport, Vermont.[10] The family lived in Newport until 1922. They then moved to Pasadena, California for a year. Soon after returning to Newport from Pasadena, the family moved to Lebanon, New Hampshire just before school started in the fall. Eleanor was twelve years old at the time. Eleanor also had the experience of living in the Northeast Kingdom environment.

Like her brother before her, she graduated from Lebanon High School. She was the valedictorian of her graduating class.[11] After graduation she attended Mount Holyoke College for two years. Then, she transferred to the University of Michigan. She received her Bachelor's degree from the University of Michigan in 1932. Eleanor was a member of the Delta Gamma Sorority.

On April 9, 1934, Eleanor married Albert Newman who also was a University of Michigan graduate. They were married in Lebanon, New Hampshire. Eleanor's cousin, Alice, was one of the "Ribbon Girls" in a traditional wedding. At the time of their marriage, Eleanor was a stenographer and her husband was a sports editor of the Michigan Daily and was a graduate of the class of 1934. They lived in Ann Arbor, Michigan, when they were first married.[12] Soon after they were married they moved to New York City, since Albert became a writer for Newsweek magazine. Their son, John, was born on October 7, 1940. Albert then became a foreign correspondent as war broke out in Europe.

One event that Al Newman covered for Newsweek was the unfortunate incident that General George Patton caused in the Sicily campaign near Messina in 1943. The general accosted a young man both orally and physically calling him a coward. In fact the young man was ill.

General Patton was a brilliantly aggressive field commander. He was also impetuous and likely to be out of control, in short, a loose cannon. General Omar Bradley, who was General Patton's commanding officer, convinced Al Newman and other national correspondents to hold the story. Later, an expose-seeking reporter named Drew Pearson got wind of the incident and caused a dramatic reaction at home.

Newman also witnessed the freeing of a Nazi concentration camp in 1944. He saw the emaciated figures of several hundred Jewish detainees and the evidence of 1,000 deaths at the hands of the Germans. Then, in 1945, Al Newman was involved in an incident of a German general claiming to be a count who wanted to surrender and disavow any connection to Nazism. This act of disavowal was a common practice among Germans as they saw the reign of Nazism collapsing.[13]

Meanwhile, Eleanor was at home raising John alone. She was living in New York possibly because John's paternal grand parents were there. Al Newman's father was a professor at New York University. Unfortunately, Eleanor and Albert Newman were divorced in 1945. World War II presented a strain on families, and many families were broken as a result.

She worked as a buyer for Lord and Taylor, a Fifth Avenue department store. She was the organizer and manager of the Five-Four Shop in New York. She deserves credit for the initiative she had to exercise to obtain such an important job. With a young boy to rear and the climate of the times to face, she needed to have a strong personality.

In 1958, Eleanor married Victor Borella. The marriage took place in the Governor's Mansion in Concord, New Hampshire. Victor was the executive vice president of Rockefeller Center and aide to Governor Rockefeller of New York.[14]

Eleanor was the first woman in our branch of the family to receive a degree from a four-year college. The flair for marketing that she inherited from her father proved an advantage for her.

In the thirteen years between her divorce from Albert Newman and her marriage to Victor Borella, Eleanor raised John alone. She also worked as a professional woman in a society that didn't always accord women the support they needed.

Eleanor died in 1975 in New Canaan, New Hampshire. Her obituary indicated that she was a director of the Currier Company in Lebanon, New Hampshire. She also had other community and charitable affiliations.

Eleanor spent most of her adult life in New York City. As a result, I did not have an opportunity to know her. As I turn to my cousins, Dwight and Alice, and my sisters, Margaret and Clara, I can talk about people whom I know.

As I pointed out, I had gotten to know Lane well beginning in his mid eighties. I have heard about Eleanor but with not as much familiarity as Lane, Dwight and Alice. As I have said elsewhere in this chronicle of our family, I have just needed to ask the right questions to widen and deepen my knowledge of each of these interesting people.

Dwight Dwinell, son of Carl Dwinell, was born in Orleans, Vermont, March 11, 1912.[15] Orleans is a small community in the northwestern portion of the Northeast Kingdom of Vermont. Dwight was a very proud product of that society. Dwight's parents were Carl and Kate Dwinell, my aunt and uncle.

The family lived on School Street near the center of town across the street from Dwight's grand aunt, Irene. The family referred to her as Aunt Rene. I thought that use of her name was peculiar to my father. However, I noticed in Lane's diary that occasionally Aunt Rene would visit their Newport home.

I remember that both houses had distinctive front porches, and they were near a school with a large schoolyard. These homes are where we would visit on our trips to Vermont.

Dwight was a very likable person. He was tall for his generation, slightly over six feet. His father, Carl, was quite tall, as was my father. They were both about five feet, eleven inches, about my height at my tallest. It is interesting to note that my grandfather, Dwight, my uncle Dean and his son, Lane, were quite short while Dwight, his father, my father and me are relatively tall for our generations.

Dwight played basketball in college, Worcester Polytechnic Institute. His height probably helped him at this game. He majored in mechanical engineering at the Institute.

When Dwight graduated in 1932, it was not easy to find a job. His first job was for the Fisher Underwood Company, manufacturers of typewriters. He then worked as a mechanical engineer for the Sylvania Corporation. His father indicated that Dwight worked in the light bulb facility of Sylvania. During World War II, he worked on an important bomb project out of this light-bulb division. This facility was responsible for the development and production of parts for one of the most powerful bombs used in the War.[16] Dwight was instrumental in developing patents connected with the production of Magicubes. Magicubes were used as flash bulb devices on small cameras, thus popularizing the use of flash cameras in amateur photography. Dwight's patents were in the development of production equipment to produce the ultimate finished goods.

He had twelve patents in total. Some of the patents that Dwight developed in collaboration with his engineering colleagues during the 1950s and 1960s include the following:

Process and Apparatus for Coating Rods
Electric Lamp
Cane Coating Apparatus
Lamp Basing Machinery
Article Feeding Apparatus
Lead Wire Feed Mechanism

Each of these inventions had a specific production-oriented application in the development of a specific product for Sylvania. In 1976 Dwight received a $10,000 award for the development of production equipment, the Equipment Award. Dwight started his career with Sylvania in 1936. He retired in 1973. He was the manager of equipment design at the company's Equipment Development Plant in Salem, Massachusetts. He had a 37-year career with the Sylvania Company.[17]

Dwight was a very confident but quietly friendly man. He spent most of his adult life living in Reading, Massachusetts. When he retired he moved to Brownington, Vermont. Brownington is immediately north of Orleans about five miles from Canada.

When our son, John, was ready to go to college, he wanted to be an engineer. He wasn't sure what type of engineer he wanted to be. I suggested that my wife, Ann, John and I visit Dwight in Brownington.

As John posed the question to Dwight the response was that John should not worry about the specifics of undergraduate training. Dwight indicated that he wanted to be an aeronautical engineer but he stated "Who needed an aeronautical engineer in 1932?"

Dwight married Mabel Atkins Miller on July 28, 1945. Mabel was very active as a leader in the Fellowship of Congregational Women. She was also a high school social studies teacher in Connecticut as well as Lexington, Massachusetts. She was graduated from Mount Holyoke College in 1928 with an A. B. degree and received a M. A. degree from the University of Iowa in 1933.[18]

Along with their considerable professional accomplishments, Dwight and Mabel were very active in the Congregational Church. This activity allowed them to travel a great deal. They made excellent ambassadors for this religion as solid practitioners of community and religious life.

There are two stories that help describe Dwight as a person. First, when I was eleven years old, I went to my grandfather's funeral in Montpelier, Vermont, in February of 1940. During a lull in the reception after the service, Dwight took me out on a hill of Dwinell Street, named after my grandfather.

There were kids skiing and coasting on a substantial hill nearby. Dwight was in his late twenties but seemed willing to be with this kid from Massachusetts to the south. After a few minutes he said, "How do you feel?" I replied "OK." Dwight looked at me and said "How cold do you think it is?" I said "Oh, about 25." He then said "I better get you inside; it's 20 below." He knew that Lowell, Massachusetts, would be warmer at 25 degrees but more humid. It would actually feel colder in Lowell. He knew it would be dangerous for a kid from southern New England to stay out any longer in the Vermont cold. He knew Vermont.

Secondly, Ann and I visited Dwight and Mabel at their retirement home in Brownington for the first time before John came with us. Their home was on a long, dirt road directly north of Brownington Center. Soon after we arrived Dwight said, "Did you have any trouble finding us?" Ann replied "No, Al always knows where he is in Vermont." With a twinkle in his eyes Dwight replied "Oh, I don't think I'd have any trouble getting him lost." In a few minutes while Mabel was preparing lunch, he took us for a ride toward Derby and Derby Line at the Canadian border. I was soon lost.

When we returned to the lunch Mabel had prepared, Dwight showed us the home he had built to their specifications. His picture window in the living room was situated so that you could see Mount Mansfield, about fifty miles to the southwest. Jay Peak was about ten or fifteen miles west. The Laurentian Mountains in Quebec were about fifty miles north. The window was perfectly placed for this scene.

He then showed us two closets. One closet reached from the floor to the ceiling. It was exactly deep enough so that a person could not put one can behind another. It would be easier to find the can you needed this way. The other closet was exactly deep, long and wide enough to hold the leaf to the dining-room table. This was an engineer at work who had a penchant for Yankee utility.

Although Dwight spent most of his adult life living in Reading, Massachusetts, and working in Salem, Massachusetts, he was a product of the Northeast Kingdom of Vermont. This humble but confident man had a strong sense of who he was. As I recall the other players in this saga of Vermont, I can see the Vermont spirit in this quietly competent man.

Dwight's sister, Alice Julia Dwinell, was born in Orleans, Vermont, on July 13, 1913.[19] She spent most of her career living in Quincy, Massachusetts. In our direct line of descent of the Dwinell family members who have lived in America, Alice has the greatest longevity.

It is obvious when you talked with Alice for any length of time that she is a proud member of the Northeast Kingdom. She had an encyclopedic knowledge of the Dwinell family. As in any family, the Vermont contingent of the Dwinell clan has an intricate web of surnames related by marriage. She had a remarkable capacity to identify these entities.

Whenever I talked with Alice about the Dwinell clan, I needed to get out a road map of Vermont to identify the areas she depicted. I remember both Alice and Dwight as the children of my Uncle Carl and Aunt Kate. Both Alice and Dwight always had a positive greeting for me at the end of that long trek from Lowell, Massachusetts, to Orleans, Vermont.

As I had gotten to know Alice better in recent years, I realized that she had an active and interesting childhood. She had told me about climbing a hill near Orleans to watch as during prohibition alcoholic beverages were smuggled across the border at Derby Line, a town at the border. When I told her that I studied the Vermont sense of independence during their years as a Republic, she accepted my version gently as the good teacher finds that her student has discovered that which she knows so well.

Vermont was admitted to statehood in 1791. The delay despite Vermont's contribution to the Revolutionary War was due to the competing land claims of the states of New York and New Hampshire. During this time, Vermont was an independent republic. The residents of Vermont retained that sense of independence and have passed it down through the generations.[20]

As Vermont developed, first, as the New Hampshire Grants under English and the New Hampshire Colony control, then, as the Republic, a western movement of settlers was occurring. Vermont was that sparsely populated frontier to the north. As Vermont was bypassed even after it acquired statehood, its independence continued. As the War of 1812 loomed, Vermonters were a long way in distance and awareness from the specific reasons for the conflict.

England was continuing to maintain a sphere of influence in their former colony, particularly in trade. One of the specific courses of action of the United States as a result of the diplomatic conflict leading to war was to boycott British goods. It was illegal during this period to trade with England.

Vermont's trade with England was long standing and a matter of survival. As an outpost of this new nation, Vermont sensed that the laws of trade newly enacted represented an economic threat to their somewhat separate civilization. It was the intent of Vermont citizens to sustain trade with England, and so they did. The Canadian border offered trading possibilities, since Canada was still a British Colony.

As the crow flies, it is approximately thirty miles from the Canadian border to Mount Mansfield, Vermont's highest peak. Today, as one drives from Stow, Vermont to the town of Jeffersonville, it is necessary to go through Smugglers' Notch. Smugglers' Notch is at the base of Mount Mansfield.

This notch is noted as a passageway in an otherwise rugged mountainous landscape. It is also noted for possessing a labyrinth of caves on its steep slopes. This notch received its name from the illicit trade of the War of 1812 era that helped keep the Vermont economy alive.

I learned this information about northern Vermont as I was first studying the Dwinell Vermont heritage. Alice knew I was studying this history, especially when I asked so many questions—so many that were quite naïve to her.

When she told me of her view from the hill of the "Rum Runners" of the Prohibition Era, I asked her if these illicit purveyors of alcoholic beverages used Smugglers' Notch to stash their merchandise. Her answer was a laconic "Yes." Evidently, her student was doing well.

Alice attended the Graded School of Orleans and graduated from Orleans High School in 1931. She then attended Wheelock College for three years until 1934. Wheelock College was a normal school; a three-year college designed to provide teaching credentials for beginning teachers. Her education would continue, first in Columbia University in New York and then in Boston University where she received a Bachelor's degree and then a master's degree.

Her career as a teacher began in the summer of 1934.[21] She was a Nursery Kindergarten teacher in Hardwick, Vermont. She then taught in the Orleans Graded School in Grades 2 and 3 from 1934 to 1937. I have a 1935 contract from the Orleans, Vermont, school system awarding Alice a stipend of $612 per year as a second grade teacher.

After her Orleans experience, she worked in the Springfield, Vermont, school system in grade 1 and 2 from 1939 until 1944. Alice had an interesting educational experience in the North School of the Springfield system. A plan was instituted wherein teachers were asked to continue to teach students they had in the first grade as these students progressed through the grades to grade eight. So, at one point in her Springfield career Alice was a teacher of grades 7 and 8 English.

She explained to me that this task took place after she taught grades 1 and 2 during the morning. Any one with any teaching experience would realize that this teaching load is a remarkable preparatory challenge.

After her Springfield experience, Alice became a grade 1 teacher in the Burlington, Vermont Schools for the 1945–46 school years. She then moved to Massachusetts in 1946 to begin a long career as a grade 1 teacher in the Milton Public Schools.

Alice retired in 1979 after 45 years of teaching. She then lived in an assisted living facility in Quincy, Massachusetts. Even then, she was a leader among this group of people. She belonged to several action groups including the cable show on local television. Quiet leadership has marked her life.

Alice passed away on April 21, 2006. She was 92 years, 9 months and 8 days old. She had set an enviable record for longevity in our direct Dwinell line of descent.

As is the case with her brother, Dwight, this account is just an outline of the life of this person. Hopefully, as we consider the Vermont experience of our ancestors, this account of Alice's life will show a spirit that is uniquely Vermont oriented. Next, I need to explore my generation of the nuclear Dwinell family from Lowell, Massachusetts.

Our beginning as a nuclear family in Lowell was at 93 Westford Street. This address is part of a rather large apartment complex on the edge of the downtown section of the city. My older sister, Margaret, was born at this address on January 20, 1923. The family was to live in this apartment until six months after I was born. In June 1929, we moved to a three-bedroom house in an industrial neighborhood near the outskirts of Lowell, 98 Sayles Street.

Margaret always had a wide variety of interests and was an excellent student. She was, and still is, an inveterate collector. I always had to be careful, for example, not to disturb her rock collection on the foundation ledge adjacent to the cellar stairs. She was a very enthusiastic Girl Scout, so she was always saving something toward one Merit Badge or another.

Our dining arrangements were informal except that I was strategically placed next to Margaret. She took on the task of civilizing me. She managed to get my elbows off the table, but I recall that it took some time before I held a fork correctly. Like most families, we had a rule that no one left the table until everyone was finished eating. Since I had another agenda, I could be very efficient in the art of completing a meal. Margaret was directed toward the pleasures of dining.

Margaret was a devotee of the Dagwood Bumpstead School of dining. A comic strip entitled "Blondie" had a male character that would make a sandwich of everything on the typical dinner plate. Margaret followed his lead. By the time that I was finished eating my meal, Margaret would have just completed the erection of her masterpiece. The house rules indicated that I was to remain. Sometimes, mercifully, mother would intervene. Margaret did help me in other ways, not as dogmatically as at mealtime.

These dining rules applied to the evening meal, only. Our father came home for lunch with the company truck, so he could get back to work or run a company errand. He didn't have much time and needed a large meal, since he worked hard. We would have a hearty meal in a relaxed environment.

Margaret was always an excellent student with many interests. When we got the piano from our grandfather, she took lessons for awhile. Not only did she excel at school, but also she was always avidly interested in a variety of pastimes.

She graduated from Lowell High School in 1940. She pursued a college-commercial course of studies with four years of Latin among her college-bound subject matter electives. Despite this rigorous academic load, Margaret graduated ninth in a graduating class of 900.

She was certainly college material, but our father did not believe it was practical for a young woman to pursue a college education. He wanted her to pursue a career with more immediate rewards. The recent Depression that America was trying to pull out of may have influenced his decision.

Margaret took the appropriate Civil Service Examination for federal service. As a result, she was able to accept a position in the Office of the Chief of the Bureau of Naval Personnel in Washington, D.C. She was able to tell us some very interesting stories of her experiences although some of her knowledge was secret, even top secret.

For example, Margaret was accustomed to seeing naval officers being moved from ship to ship, even from one sector or ocean to another in this multi-continental war. There was one oft-repeated placement that puzzled her. Certain naval officers kept being transferred to the Manhattan Project. She knew of the location of many fleets and had a good understanding of what was happening, but this placement baffled her. When she told me of this mystery years later, I was reassured that we can keep a secret when we really need to. The Manhattan Project was the name given to the organization effort to produce the Atomic Bomb.

There was one occasion when she needed to have access to top secret documents. Margaret was cleared for secret but not top secret. Her commanding officer informed her, first, but she soon found herself under armed Marine guard as she perused the top-secret documents in order to do her job. She also learned that the word loran was secret and should not be used in normal conversation. Today, we know that this is routine equipment on any ocean-going vessel.

Margaret left Washington in 1948 to return to Lowell. She accepted a position in Boston as the secretary to the chief psychiatrist of the Veteran's Administration in Boston. Actually, she found herself being the secretary to a substantial staff of psychiatrists.

While in the Veterans' Administration, she started her career as a student at Boston College. Her academic work was completed mainly at the Boston In-Town College. She received her A. B. from Boston College in 1954. Margaret then studied social work at Boston University and received her MSW (Master's Degree in Social Work) in 1956.

Her career as a social worker began at the Boston State Hospital soon after she received her master's degree. This institution was a mental hospital. As she worked in this environment she began to acquire a good reputation as a psychiatric social worker.

After the state hospital experience, Margaret was employed at Center Club. Center Club was a vocational rehabilitation program designed to mainstream recently released mental patients that had been institutionalized. She advocated and soon initiated a cooperative housing venture called Center House. This house was a multi story apartment house near Andrews Square in South Boston.

Margaret employed her considerable social work skill as she assumed the role of the self-styled land lady for the Center Club clientele who would benefit from this experience. Margaret had one rule for her tenants—"Don't act lazy or crazy."

Margaret worked in this role for several decades. She became a reliable advocate for this population and was sought out by the local business and government leaders of South Boston including the judges and officials at the South Boston District Court. She was an effective community leader as well as an effective professional resource.

Margaret retired in the late 1990s and moved about two miles away to a condominium apartment in the Savin Hill neighborhood of Dorchester. One of her South Boston friends was concerned for her, because she was moving so far away.

We celebrated her eightieth birthday recently. People from South Boston were glad to see her. Soon after her birthday, record breaking low temperatures hit Boston. My wife and I were concerned for Margaret, so we called her and got no response. We have a key, so we drove to her home. When we entered, no one was there.

We left a note, so she called later in the day. She had left in the morning to see a doctor ten miles away, so she used public transportation. When she got back, she walked about a mile to get the subway to meet our sister. The two of them went to an afternoon Boston Symphony Orchestra presentation. Then, Margaret came home. Her Northeast Kingdom Heritage served her and my sister Clara, well.

Her present avocation is the Castle Island Association. Castle Island is an historic landmark in South Boston with an impressive military history as a Revolutionary War fort. She has acted as a guide in the Fort and is one of the authorities regarding its history and significance. She is also active in South Boston Library activities.

Meanwhile, she is the grand aunt to a host of children of our eleventh generation. She knows the Dwinell family well and has been a valuable resource for me as I have attempted to answer a myriad of questions.

My younger sister, Clara, was born on July 13, 1925, at 93 Westford Street in Lowell, Massachusetts. She lived in this apartment environment until we moved to the home on Sayles Street.

Clara, too, was an excellent student and she still is a very conscientious and involved person. She was a member of the National Honor Society in high school. She worked in the community as well.

I'm sure that she knew of Margaret's experience with our father regarding college. She decided early in her high school career that she would go to college. Much to her credit, she set out to work to cover the cost.

I acquired a paper route when I was twelve years old in the summer of 1941. Clara was in high school about to start her junior year. Soon after I started the route, Clara took over part of the task. I had a bicycle by that time, so she took over the part of the total route with the most hills. She had to walk this route each morning before high school classes. This was the beginning. Actually, this was not the beginning of her money making career. Both Margaret and Clara told me that they baby sat for fifty cents a night—Margaret would make a dollar a day for this type of work.

Clara worked a variety of jobs to defray her college costs. She had a job, as a cashier in Gagnon's, a Lowell department store. Her first two years in college were during the war years, so she obtained a factory job making and then inspecting "Flying Suits" in a building we later knew as the Giant Store on Dutton Street in downtown Lowell. She had a job in a laundry in the office. If these jobs were not enough, she used the family car to transport students for a fee from Lowell to Salem to college. Some of these jobs were summer jobs, but some of the jobs were during the school year.

Clara chose a state college even though she had a good academic record and could have gone to a more expensive private college. She obtained a Bachelor of Science in Education from the State Teachers' College at Salem, Massachusetts. As a result, she became the first person in our nuclear family in the direct line of descent from our ancestors to receive a college degree.

Clara's career at Salem State, as it is called today, was interesting. She went to Salem from 1943 until 1947. The first two years were during World War II. Essentially, this co-ed college became a college of mostly women. Clara was busy excelling academically as she made the President's List each of her first three years. The President's List is equivalent to what larger colleges call the Dean's List. It meant that you maintained a favorable academic grade average.

Despite being a commuting student who had to transport her fellow students, she was busy in extra curricular activity. She served on the Publicity Committee all of her four years of college being the chairperson in her senior year. The college administration actually relied upon student committees to perform administrative roles for the college. These functions were under the control of the Student Council. So Clara had a big responsibility. She was active in athletics—basketball, field hockey, soccer, softball and volleyball. In fact, she was on the "Lowell team" in field hockey. There was a state teachers college in Lowell. Does this mean she was our family's first woman intercollegiate athlete? Her classmates recognized Clara as a leading member of the junior class when she was selected to be part of the "Daisy Chain". The "Chain" was a group of junior women who participated in the graduation ceremony.

Clara then went on to Boston University to obtain a Master's degree in Business Education. While at Boston University, she had the opportunity to work on the Evaluative Criteria for the accreditation of high schools throughout New

England. This work had been developed in 1938 and published in 1940. A revision was due for 1950. She had a staff job in this organization rather than the typical assistantship that graduate students obtain.

The Evaluative Criteria is used to determine if a high school has reached a standard necessary for accreditation. The criteria also serve as a vehicle for curriculum reform. Her graduate work and the work for the Association caused her to obtain a business teacher position in Franklin High School, Franklin, Massachusetts.

She soon became the department head of the Business Education Department. Clara was a member of the Commercial Directors of Greater Boston while serving as the Franklin High School Department Head. The Commercial Directors Club was an organization that had a great deal of influence in pedagogy and curriculum content in the field of Business Education throughout Massachusetts.

She married Ruston Lodi on August 18, 1951. Clara continued to work as a department head until 1955. She then decided to devote her life to their family that she and Ruston were creating.

Ruston Lodi had started his college career at the State Teachers College at Salem before he joined the Army at the beginning of World War II. While in the Army, Ruston was a jeep driver and interpreter for Brigadier General Edgar Erskine Hume. General Hume was a public health doctor for the Fifth Army during the Italian Campaign.

In April, 1945, the Allied Forces were approaching Modena, Italy. Ruston was born in Ferrara, Italy on June 20, 1922. Not only did Ruston know Italian but the dialect of the region. Modena and Ruston's native Ferrara are only about 20 miles apart.

At a critical juncture during the work of the General, it was necessary for Ruston to stand up in his jeep to interpret for the General using the dialect of the partisan Italians. The Italian people wanted to attack the German prisoners who were in the area. The General needed to protect these Germans. General Erskine Hume was going to be the officer in charge of the occupation of Modena. Essentially, the war had ended in Italy. The German prisoners of war had a right to be protected as they were released. The citizens of Modena and the surrounding area had other ideas.

Ruston earned the Silver Star for this action. It should be noted that Ruston's actions probably saved the General's life as well as the General's aide. Only these three men had entered the town. Ruston's activity counteracted the possible reactions of the crowd.[22]

When he returned from active duty, he attended Tufts University. He graduated from Tufts in 1948 with a Bachelor of Arts degree in History. He then attended Boston University and received a Master's degree in Education in 1949. Ruston became a teacher in the Foxborough, Massachusetts, Public Schools and later became an elementary school principal.

Clara and Ruston raised five children, Ruston, Andrea Pia, Carlo, Maria and Paula. Even though Clara left education to raise her family, she continued to be active in the community of Franklin. Clara was the Secretary of her church and a Eucharistic Minister as well. She serves on the Library Board of Directors and is a very active and influential member of the Franklin Cares group. Recently, she worked hard to support a local initiative to overcome a state imposed ceiling on local expenditures called Proposition 2 ½ in Massachusetts. This initiative to override the state-imposed ceiling was not supported by the community. As a result, the library is in danger of closing, the fire department may lose a station and the school system has suffered.[23]

The residents of Franklin are very proud of their library. The Franklin Library is the first lending library in the history of our country. It was a private library until 1981 but has survived since its creation in 1778. The task of retaining the tradition of this legacy would be something that Clara would welcome. Ruston had been a member of the Board of Directors when the library was private.

About the time that Clara started working on the paper route with me, Margaret had recently moved to Washington. Clara then assumed the unfamiliar role of big sister. It wasn't necessarily easy for her. I was somewhat independent and was accorded the freedom that the youngest in the family who happens to be a boy generally receives. But, life went on in our family and in the paper business.

Soon after we started on our paper routes, it was necessary for Clara and me to make an important business decision. We delivered three types of Boston newspapers, the Boston Post for two cents a copy and the Boston Globe and Boston Herald for three cents a copy. Some of our colleagues on other routes were charging a delivery fee—two cents extra for the Globe and Herald to round off the weekly charge to twenty cents and three cents extra for the Post to round off the charge to fifteen cents per week. Clara and I agreed that we did not want to charge this fee. We were already making a profit.

The local distributors with whom we dealt indicated that we had to charge the fee if we were to keep our route. Reluctantly, we agreed. We didn't lose many customers and the tips kept coming. Years later I learned that we were charging a regressive tax to the Post customers. One can assume that these people, for the most part, had lower incomes if they purchased the lower cost product. Thus, we were charging the lower income customers a greater per cent of the cost of the product and their income. Fortunately, there were not too many micro economists among our Post customers.

Since we delivered the Boston papers in Lowell on the outer edge of Metropolitan Boston, our customers represented only a few people on each street. Our respective routes, therefore, were rather long. On rainy winter mornings when Clara and I would have to walk through slush, dad would sometimes drive either or both of us along our route.

If the mornings were snowy or somewhat cold, we were on our own. A little snow or cold wouldn't hurt. If it were a blizzard, we would wait until the snow almost stopped. We waited only because our stacks of newspapers would not yet have been delivered.

I must admit that on normal mornings Clara would have gotten to our packs of papers first. Even then, I found it difficult to get out of bed in the morning. She would have had to take out the exact numbers of each type of paper for her route. All I had to do was to pick up what was left and be on my way. If there were a shortage of any type of paper, I would "adapt" accordingly. This was a good arrangement, because I had a more casual reaction to the possible outcomes.

There were two mornings in February, 1943, that presented a problem. The official recorded low temperature in Boston on February 9, 1943, was 18 degrees below zero. Lowell was inland and 26 miles farther north. Typically, the temperature in Lowell would be lower than Boston. We were told that it was 25 degrees below zero in Lowell on that day. I have not yet verified the Lowell temperature, but Clara and I can assure you that it was cold. Six days later the low temperature was a balmy fourteen degrees below zero in Boston.[24]

On the first of these two frigid mornings in 1943, Clara and I set out on our separate routes for our little three-hour jaunt on a pleasant, albeit, cold February morning. We knew it would be cold, so we were properly dressed, even to the scarf across our face. I received a frozen nose and frozen cheeks. I guess I wasn't very efficient in the use of the face cover.

Clara kept the scarf snug on her face, but, alas, she continued to breathe. The moistness and warmth of her breath caused moisture to form on her eyelashes. This moisture rapidly turned to icicles. We survived. In fact, six days later the morning was within only a few degrees of the same low temperatures. I walked the route without incident using the scarf more efficiently about my face. As far as I know, Clara did not have any ill effects as a result of experiencing that second frigid morning.

Dad would not have thought this temperature plunge to be anything unusual. I am sure that he realized that we would have a reaction. In his defense, he had a limited amount of gasoline to use, because of rationing. Even heating oil was rationed. Other things were rationed as well even including food. It was necessary for each family to apply for ration stamps and to husband these stamps for a variety of goods carefully. When a desirable good was not rationed, it was in short supply. I can remember mother carefully counting her stamps and planning her grocery list before heading to market.

Life in Lowell was interesting. Both Clara and I knew the bus routes well and did our share of walking in addition to the paper route. Downtown Lowell was two miles away, since we lived on the outskirts of the city. Like many New England cities, Lowell was planned so that the factory workers could easily walk to work.

I can remember walking the City when I would go to the library, then wander around to see what I could find. I still remember the Commissary lines at the closed factory on Jackson Street. The unemployed people who had run out of resources were eligible for surplus food available from the national government. The surplus food was the result of a food purchase program of the federal government designed to keep family farms across the country operating. Virtually everyone in the nation was suffering in one way or another.

The Roosevelt administration tried to help. The Congress enacted legislation to create the Works Progress Administration, WPA, and the Civilian Conservation Corps, CCC. These measures were designed to generate employment.

The WPA built roads, public buildings and libraries. Look around your town at bridges or public buildings that you think may have been build in the 1930s. You may see a plaque that mentions the WPA. I can remember a street near our home in Lowell that was created by the WPA. Competent men who needed work accomplished this effort.

The Civilian Conservation Corps, CCC, was created to employ youth to reduce idleness, generate employment and preserve and enhance natural resources. I can remember the older boys in their dark green uniforms waiting for the bus that would take them way out into the countryside. Actually, the bus ride was to Ashby near the Townsend border in north central Massachusetts. My first teaching job was in Townsend. I can remember that pleasant state park created by Lowell CCC boys in the 1930s.

Another Depression phenomenon in Lowell was the shovel brigade that shoveled the streets of Lowell after a snow storm in the 1930s. The local bus company would plow the streets that they needed. The city Department of Public Works would clear the other streets. To generate employment one winter, those streets that were the responsibility of the city were literally shoveled by hand.

Although income levels were low, or in some cases non-existent for the very poor, people managed to find a way to cope. Families found a way to let their kids have fun. We had fun in the neighborhood as well.

Some of the lesser-used streets were closed to all but residential traffic in the winter, so that we could coast. The older boys set up ski runs; coasting areas and even a toboggan run on hills which were apparently vacant.

Clara shared in the fun but also the work. We were both on the sifting of the ash detail. The house was heated with coal. We would empty the ashes from the furnace. Then, we would sift the ashes to obtain reusable coals. Every penny counted. This sifting process is somewhat like trying to stretch the use of charcoal in the barbecue today. There is one difference. We save the usable burnt charcoal to avoid a trip to the supermarket. We sifted ashes to keep the coal bill low.

The furnace we used was a steam furnace. This fact created another duty that presented a problem. To build up pressure in the furnace to force the heat upstairs to the living areas on the first and second floors, my father would close the damper. As the pressure built and the radiators became filled with steam and warmth, the steam would have no place to go. Therefore, the furnace would "blow" off steam that would fill the cellar. The first available child would then be told to go down cellar to open the damper.

I was frightened and Margaret has told me that she was frightened as well. I haven't yet solicited Clara's opinion. Since I am far from being a physicist, I still don't know why we failed to get scalded by the steam. I also don't know why the furnace didn't explode. Each time I went down those cellar stairs I felt either or both of those conditions were about to occur. For the most part, the house was warm and all the radiators were kept working.

Many families during the Depression did not have the luxury of continual heat. Many homes shut off rooms in the winter by closing rooms and turning off the steam radiator or closing the grill on the 1930s and 1940s version of a hot-air heating system. Many families did not send heat to the bedrooms, since the beds had blankets. Also, many homes had parlors as well as dens. They relaxed in the dens and closed off the parlors. The parlors were used for formal occasions, so they did not have to be heated when not in use. These heating conditions were for ordinary people who had a job. There were many people in Lowell and across the nation in abject poverty that did not have the luxury of a home or a central heating system.

As everyone did, we lived a frugal life during the Depression. Then, we lived through the rationing and shortages of products during World War II. I think that it was easier to live through World War II shortages, since the economic conditions of the Depression created the necessity for self-imposed curtailment of goods, even necessities. Clara kept her goals in mind throughout this period and emerged as a valuable professional in Franklin.

Her enthusiasm and effort has not changed. Like other members of the Dwinell family, the result of this effort is a person who has been a leader in her family and in her community.

Clara Lodi has five children and eight grandchildren. Her children are Ruston, Andrea Pia, Carlo, Maria and Paula. This is a family that has made its mark. Clara's oldest child is Ruston Lodi.

Ruston is the Director of Public Affairs of the Massachusetts Housing Partnership Fund. This organization is designed to provide housing to communities by helping them conceptualize the most effective plan for their needs. The role of the organization is to help communities develop their own plans. Ruston's role is to provide information and materials to local officials and news outlets in the most effective way possible. The web site noted as the reference to this explanation of Ruston's role is one of his most effective tools.[25]

Ruston is a graduate of Colby College. Before starting a second career with the Massachusetts Housing Partnership Fund, he was very successful as a reporter and editor for the Metro West Daily News. He started his career with the Middlesex Daily News as a sports writer and, then, a sports editor. He soon became the news editor, managing editor and, then, editor of this paper. The paper evolved from the Middlesex News to the Metro West Daily News during his tenure. While Ruston was editor, the paper was twice chosen as New England Newspaper of the Year.

Ruston met his future wife, Elizabeth Gruber, at Colby College. Elizabeth Gruber Lodi is a bank executive with the Bank of America in Boston. She has a demanding role in the bank but is a relaxed and involved parent of three very active and happy children. Hannah and Rachel are two teen aged young women who are accomplished students in a challenging school system, Newton, Massachusetts. Ruston, Jr., is all boy and "competes" well with his very competent sisters. Ruston and Elizabeth have created a relaxed yet intellectual and challenging environment.

Andrea Pia Silbert is Clara's oldest daughter. She is the mother of Seth, Abby and Neal. They are very active and excellent models of well-cared-for children.

Pia, as she is known in the family, is married to Stuart Silbert. Stuart is an independent small businessperson, currently competing in several business fields.

Pia is a graduate of Springfield College. She had enjoyed a brief teaching career before marriage. Other than providing a very positive home environment, Pia has been the big sister to the Lodi family as her sisters have experienced the challenge of military service during a stressful era.

Carlo is Clara's second oldest boy. He is a graduate of Norwich University in Vermont. Carlo works as an environmental engineer. As such, he has the challenging task of traveling frequently as he visits problematical environmental sites across the country. Carlo is married to Linda who is an accomplished web-site designer.

Lieutenant Colonel Maria Lodi Barrett is stationed currently in the White House. She has experience in the first Gulf War when she was stationed in Saudi Arabia. Maria is a graduate of Tufts University. She is married to Lt. Colonel Brian Barrett who is currently stationed in the Pentagon.

Lieutenant Colonel Paula Vance has had several tours of duty in Iraq. She has been stationed in Baghdad and elsewhere. She is a graduate of Rutgers University. Paula had the unenviable task of working in the area of personnel planning in a woefully undermanned military campaign. Paula is married to Henry Vance. Henry is a retired Command Sergeant Major. His last tour of duty was in Far East Headquarters in South Korea. Recently, both Henry and Paula had tours of duty in Iraq. After retirement, Henry worked for a civilian organization contracted by the Defense Department.

Paula and Henry have two children. Their two daughters are McKenzie and Meredeth. Henry has done an excellent job of caring for their daughters while Paula carries out her tour of duty.

Clara is still quite busy with this active family. She still lives in Franklin and has a right to be proud of the contributions she has made. Her calm exterior belies the fact that she has understandable concern for her military daughters.

I was born on December 19, 1928, at 93 Westford Street as well. We moved to Sayles Street the following June. Our new surroundings were a good place for a boy to grow up.

These were the Depression years, so everyone was frugal. Our family was reasonably well off, because our father was a factory foreman who worked five and one half days each week. There was unemployment around us, though, and we learned to be thrifty. Part of that thriftiness was my father's Yankee background. As will be evident, part of this thriftiness was the life my father had to lead before he came to Lowell.

I did a great deal of walking as a boy and got to know the city well. As my father took me to sand lot baseball games and to a radio store that he used to frequent, I remembered the routes. Also, I read a great deal, so I would walk to the library in the center of the city.

My first gainful employment was at age eleven. I had a friend named Tommy Duffy. His father owned a variety store at the intersection of Branch and Middlesex Streets in Lowell at the foot of Dover Street. I sorted soda bottles for redemption for the princely sum of ten cents per hour. When you break down the hours, this pay was comparable to the babysitting pay that my sisters received.

That summer, my duties expanded. Mr. Duffy had built a small stand for the sale of fireworks. Tommy and I were to man the stand. In those days, practically every man smoked openly in public. As the men approached the stand, they would be smoking. This was a typical condition, so I thought nothing of the practice.

However, Tommy and I were standing among considerable firepower. If a spark from one of those cigarettes hit a salute in our booth, Tommy and I would still be in orbit. We did collect our ten cents an hour and learned that there is risk in a capitalist society.

At age 12 I acquired the paper route soon to be shared with Clara. Soon after I started on the route before Clara joined me, I came into the house late one afternoon. My mother said to me "Your father wants to talk to you." When I went into the living room where he usually sat, he said "There is a bicycle waiting for you in the Bicycle Shop." I said "Thank you." Every boy in Lowell knew about this store in downtown Lowell.

The next day I walked down town to get my bike. We lived in the Highlands section of the city a gradual two-mile climb away from the center of the city. When I arrived, the sales person was happy to give me my bicycle. It was a Columbia two wheeler, not quite the best but solid, a product my father would buy. Then, I was ready to head home.

I did have a slight problem. I had never ridden a two-wheel bicycle. I learned as I pedaled those two miles. When I walked in the back door, my mother said, "You know you owe him the money." I didn't know this, but I replied "I know." It took me about six months to pay him back. No one told me how much I would owe, since all parties to the transaction realized that a twelve-year old boy can read a price tag. The price tag read $33. How did my father find $33? This practice of the repayment of an expenditure would be common for the children in families in those times.

I was a reasonably good student but rather casual compared to Margaret and Clara. My academic record was promising until my sophomore year in high school. I became chronically ill and my academic record suffered. I did manage to graduate from Lowell High School in 1946. Then, I went to work full time as an assistant manager trainee in the motion picture theatre business. After a year in this role, I decided to go back to school. I wanted to go to a two-year college to become an accountant.

First, I went back to high school for a post graduate year to become acclimated to school again. By this time I was ready to study. A high school teacher named Edward Sullivan approached me and convinced me to attend the State Teachers College at Salem. His reasoning was the tuition was low, I would receive a degree and I could decide between teaching and the business world after I had received a four year degree. Since my grades were deficient, I needed to pass an entrance examination. I was accepted. I knew that Clara had gone to Salem, but that did not influence my decision either way. Throughout my school career I had been compared to Margaret and Clara. It was tough to have two brilliant sisters. Salem accepted me for whom I proved to be. I learned from that experience and remembered this as a teacher later.

The Salem experience is what I needed. I even survived the study of Shorthand and Typewriting, otherwise doing rather well. As a result I obtained a Bachelor of Science in Education in 1952. After having accepted two draft deferments to finish my degree, I was drafted into the Korean War. Ultimately, I served in Japan at Yokohama Army Hospital with temporary duty to Korea and the United States to process repatriated prisoners from the Chinese prison camps as the war ended. These vicarious experiences gave me a lesson as to the ravages of war.

In July 1954, I was separated from the Army. Then, I started my teaching career in Townsend High School, Townsend, Massachusetts, in September. Townsend was a rural community. I taught eight classes in six class periods. My extra duties included being the co-advisor to the Junior Class, the Advisor to the Student Council, at one time the Advisor to the Cheerleaders, and since I had the only mimeograph in the school I started the school's first student paper. I had the privilege of doing all this for $2,800 per year. It was fun. In my second year at Townsend in February, 1956, I started an MBA program at Northeastern University.

Ann Jones and I were married on December 23, 1956. In September 1957, I began my career at Brookline High School, Brookline, Massachusetts. After the first year I was able to specialize in my academic strengths, Economics, Accounting and Business Administration. I received my MBA from Northeastern University in 1959. I then went on to receive an Advanced Certificate in Educational Administration from Boston College in 1968 and an A.M. in Economics from the University of Illinois in 1971.

These degrees allowed me to help the underachieving economically disadvantaged students of an otherwise very rich community. The degrees also allowed me to teach economic theory and business administration subject matter to college-bound students. During the evenings, I pursued the dual career of college teaching in Economics, Accounting and Business Administration. This college work was mainly at Framingham State College.

I retired from Brookline High School in 1991. I then began teaching part time and, at times, full time in the day school of Framingham State College. This work prolonged my career until 2003.

As my career progressed, our family was growing. Ann had graduated from Lowell High School in 1953. As a college-business student in high school, she had an excellent academic record. She started her career working as a secretary for the John Hancock Insurance Company in Boston. She resigned from this job as we began to have a family.

When our youngest son, John, started school so did Ann, at the college level. She was 32. Her work at Framingham State College was mainly in the Continuing Education Program as she raised a family as a homemaker and worked part time, often full time. She received a B. A. in English from Framingham State College in June 1972. She started her career as a Learning Disabilities Specialist in the Public Schools of Marlborough in September of 1972. Through all of this activity, she remained the heart of our family. The four children of ours have grown to adulthood with their own families and have retained the heart their mother provided.

As her career progressed at Marlborough, she obtained a Master's degree in Special Education from Lesley College in 1974. After a successful career at Marlborough, she accepted a position as a Core Chairperson for the Public Schools of Malden, Massachusetts. Due to budgetary constraints these core-chairperson positions were eliminated, so Ann continued her career as a Learning Disabilities Specialist.

She soon returned to college and obtained her PhD in Educational Administration from Boston College in 1991. Ann continued as a Learning Disabilities Teacher until her retirement in 2002. Her thirty-year career was marked by a consistently excellent reputation as a diagnostician and advocate for children with learning disabilities. She also became the first person in her nuclear Jones family and the nuclear Dwinell family lines of descent to earn a Ph.D. After retirement, she was substituting on both a temporary and permanent basis as needed in the same capacity as a learning disabilities specialist. Her most important job is as an accomplished and loving grandmother of ten children. Now, this occupies most of her time and interest.

Ann and I have had four children and have led an active and productive life. We can relax, now, as we travel and enjoy our cottage at Lake Winnipesaukee as well as our grand children.

Our oldest child is Theresa. She has taken on the challenge of being a corporate wife. As corporations created branch manufacturing plants across America, young upwardly mobile executives have had to travel as they received promotional opportunities. This condition has been in existence since the 1920s. Increasingly, it is a way of corporate life.

Theresa has two children. Vincent is age 14 and will be entering high school next year. Harrison is age eight and will be entering the second grade.

Our second child and oldest boy is Joseph Dwinell. He has a long career as a reporter and editor in the Boston area. Joe had worked with his cousin, Ruston Lodi, at the Metro West Daily News serving as a reporter, Bureau Chief, and then Managing Editor. He has several years of television experience reporting on suburban news and has received several awards for his reporting and editorial work.

He is currently the Executive City Editor-Web of the Boston Herald. This role has given him considerable national exposure on television network news broadcasts as a result of the sensational Entwistle case emanating in Hopkinton, Massachusetts as well as other breaking news stories. His daily blog continues to give him a national presence. Recently, his blog supported the Guardian Angel effort to combat crime in Boston. In fact, Joe was able to use his editorial leadership to allow the leadership of the Guardian Angels to communicate with the people of Boston. This helped as a serious crime wave was abated for a time, and the people were reassured that peace would return.

Joe has a bachelor's degree in English/communications from North Adams State College and a master's degree in print journalism from Boston University. He has over twenty years experience in the newspaper business.

Joe's wife, Paula, has a Bachelor's degree from North Adams State College. While being the principal homemaker for Joe and their three children, Paula has had a successful career as a social work administrator. She is the facilitator for a population of special needs people in need of intervention and support.

They have three children. Joseph is our oldest grand child. He will be entering his first year of college in September. Kaila will be a junior in high school in September. Ryan will be entering the sixth grade.

Our second oldest son, Richard, is an accomplished artist like his great grandfather, Dwight. He has a Bachelor of Fine Arts from Salem State College and has completed graduate work in web design at the Rhode Island School of Design. As Richard follows a career as a teacher for the economically disadvantaged youth in need of intervention, he is pursuing a part-time career in web design. He has several clients and is building a solid reputation. His wife, Carla, is an accomplished artistic photographer. She is pursuing a Fine Arts degree specializing in photography.

Richard and Carla have two children, Emma and Charles. Emma is an enthusiastic fourth grader and accomplished young lady with an interest in dancing and acting. Charlie is all boy. Charlie will be entering the second grade in the fall.

Our youngest son, John, is a software engineer with a solid career. He already holds five patents in the areas of pollution detection devices and barcode recognition software. He has several patents pending. As I searched the web, I discovered that he is now part of the references used by the Patent Office when searching to see if like patent applications represent new ideas.[26]

His present company is doing well as they provide barcode-scanning devices for the package shipping industry. As the American Director of Engineering for Sick, the German parent company, John is providing strong leadership. John has a Bachelor's degree in Computer Science from Framingham State College and a Master's degree in Computer Science from Boston University.

His job, now, entails more than engineering. He spends a good deal of his time trouble shooting his various products at customer sites for United Parcel Service, Federal Express, the DHL Company and other facilities across the United States and, often, in foreign countries. He also needs to attend management meetings in Germany on behalf of the American subsidiary.

John's wife, Pamela, is a Tufts University graduate with both a Bachelor and Master's degree who enjoys an impressive career as an environmental control officer and consultant for the Polaroid Corporation.

They have three children, Julia, Justin and Joshua. Julia is entering the third grade, Justin is busy in pre-school and Joshua is our youngest grandchild holding his own in this large, extended family.

My cousin, Lane, had an impressive career. He was the oldest of this generation of our family, and he was in the public light. It was easy to write about him, although it was difficult to delimit the content.

His sister and his cousins were successful as resourceful and competent people as well. Although our careers were less public, we were effective and no less important to the mission we served. Each of us had a chance to become well educated.

What was it that gave us the drive to succeed? My cousins had fathers who were a success in the business world despite having only a high school education. Perhaps this success had an effect on their children.

My father did not have the advantage of success in the business world in the conventional sense. He was an ordinary working man, but with a tremendous sense of pride and confidence. He passed that pride and confidence on to his children and grandchildren.

Where did this confidence come from? For that matter, where did the confidence come from that made my two uncles successes in business. As we have seen, these three brothers were the product of a seven-generation farming legacy. Perhaps the Dwinell experiences and the farming legacy produced a heritage that gave them the strength to succeed, even in a non farming environment, and, by extension, gave our generation this same strength to succeed in fields requiring a more academic background.

The confidence to succeed in life comes from more than a college education. There are tradition and family lessons to learn as well. We have this tradition. The eleventh generation is rapidly obtaining this tradition as well.

Conclusion

○ ○

"With nothing on it for the flame to kill
Save one who moved and was alone up there
To loom before the chaos and the glare
As if he were the last god going home
Unto his last desire

—*Edward Arlington Robinson*
"The Man Against the Sky"

The theme of this book has been the independence of the characters that have emerged. It is understandable given the circumstances the early generations faced and the life the Vermont descendants chose.

I have attempted to capture this sense of independence as I related their experience on the farms they tended or on the battlefields they experienced. They shared this sense of independence with their neighbors and their fellow soldiers as they fought for the right to be free and then fashioned the independent society that followed their success.

I have chosen to follow only one line of descent of this remarkable family for an understandable reason. Sometime in the late 1950s a man named Ira Dwinell visited our home when Ann and I were living in Millis, Massachusetts, with two of our soon to be four children. He was selling his genealogy. We could have purchased the entire work that he had accomplished or just the part that captured our direct line of descent to Mikal Donnell. We chose the direct line of descent.

I read and reread it over the years and became fascinated with the scope of history these ordinary men experienced. Our lives were busy, but this material was always in the back of my mind. When I retired in 1992, I found time to concentrate on a set of narratives that would tell the story I have just related. I have spent the last fifteen years researching this collection of materials.

There is no reason to believe that my direct line of descent is any more significant than another line of descent of the Dwinell clan that started in America so many centuries ago. We have met some of these other Dwinell family members who have touched the lives of the characters of these episodes. In chronological order, we should mention here some of the other notable Dwinell family members who should be given some notice.

Michael Dwinell, Jr.'s brother Jacob managed to start a family whose descendants managed to stay in Topsfield for 354 years. They are still living on Salem Road on the original land acquired by Mikal Donnell. Israel Dwinell's name is notable in Topsfield's contribution to the Colonial Wars.

There are two other people named Solomon Dwinell who made a contribution. Solomon Dwinell of Millbury, Massachusetts, fought in several important battles of the Revolutionary War and kept a diary of his experiences during this time. I have read this diary and found it of interest. It is said by some that Solomon mentions his Irish heritage in this diary. This Irish reference was not found in the portion of the diary that I read but the account of life in the war was of interest.

Solomon Ashley Dwinell does claim to have an Irish heritage. He has been quoted as saying that he has an Irish background. Solomon Ashley Dwinell helped settle Wisconsin as he served as a Congregational minister for many years. He was an abolitionist who was very active in the Underground Railroad activity prior to the Civil War.

I have mentioned Carlos Dwinell who fought in so many battles of the Civil War. An entire book could easily be devoted to his wartime experiences. Carlos is a descendant of the Michael Dwinell who died as the result of fighting in the Quebec area during the Colonial Wars. Michael was Benjamin Dwinell's brother.

In the Chapter on Thomas Dwinell, his brother Jonathan Dwinell who fought beside his brother at Bunker Hill was mentioned. As you review the book, The History of Topsfield, Massachusetts, so often cited in the endnotes to this book, you will see other Dwinell family members who have served their community and their country. Our contributions have gone beyond Topsfield.

I have said as I have developed this book that all I had to do was raise a question and the answers would appear. My travels have taken me to the various locales mentioned in the book, but I have been in touch with members of the Dwinell family in many other parts of the United States. The power of the internet causes people of like mind to communicate.

This communication has led me to believe that there is a chance for the entire Dwinell story to be told. People who have communicated with me have been no less interested in our heritage than I and have been a remarkable source of knowledge. I would encourage these Dwinell family members to tell their story. In fact, I would encourage anyone with a family story to explore all of its dimensions and relate what they feel is important.

Other Dwinell family members would ask different questions. As a result, their contribution would have a different emphasis. This difference would show different perspectives than my perspective.

Genealogies are important. We need to understand family relationships. The further back in time this effort takes us the better. However, there is a limitation to the family tree type of genealogical investigation. There is not enough space to tell the story the accuracy and thoroughness of a good genealogy would provide.

Ira Dwinell has done a remarkable job. His genealogy is accurate and thorough. He did provide some family information that acted as an outline for me to tell these stories. I would commend to anyone who would tell a generational story of their branch of the Dwinell clan the revised version of Ira's work written by Frank Dwinell. There are other family collections in libraries across America waiting for the story teller to use.

When I studied the concept of the history of man in the National Geographic Genographic Project materials, I realized that genealogies are male dominated. The ancestry of a family is carried through a common surname. This history is also carried through a common gene, the Y chromosome. If we were to follow the mitochondrial chromosome, the story would be far different

I have said too little of the women in the story of the Dwinell family as it has progressed through history. The story from a woman's perspective would be a remarkable contribution. What would the story of Mary's Roses tell us?

As we face a new century and millennium, our perspective will be different than the views of our ancestors from so many centuries ago. But, there is a tradition of independence and community that provides us with a direction. We learn from our ancestors and build on the tradition. These episodes are my contribution to the lessons that can be learned from one branch of one family.

Tell your family story. The world will be the better for your contribution.

Endnotes

Chapter One:

1. Johnson, Edward, Captain, "Wonder-Working Providence of Sion's Saviour in New England", London, 1654, p. 15

2. Dunnell, Henry Gale, "True Genealogy of the Dunnel and Dwinell Family", Charles Robinson, New York, 1862

3. Ipswich Deeds, pages 185–187, 1672, Grantor: Francis Pabody, Grantee: Michal Donnell (The Ipswich Deeds that are available at the Essex County Registry of Deeds in Salem, Massachusetts are a copy of the originals; therefore, signatures are not available.

4. Dwinell, Frank, Preface to the "Dwinell Genealogy Reprint and Revision, 1974

5. "Passengers to Virginia" *in Passengers to America*, p. 82

6. Ingalls, Ruth Rebecca Dwinell, Telephone Conversation, 1997. Also, Towne, John Henry, *The Houses and Buildings of Topsfield*, Topsfield Historical Society, 1902

7. Boston Globe Newspaper Article, 1939

8. Cutter, William Richard, *New England Families*, p. 1932

9. Dow, *History of Topsfield*, p. 37

10. Hayes, Carlton, J.H., *Modern Europe to 1870*, The Macmillan Company, New York, 1961, p. 119

11. Dow, *History of Topsfield*, p. 257

12. Apparent consensus of some members of the Topsfield Historical Society, July, 2003

13. Dow, *History of Topsfield*, p. 37

14. Dwinell, Ira, *Dwinell Genealogy*. I have used this source extensively throughout the book. I have not provided page numbers, because my copy only includes my direct line of descent. Page numbers were not included. This source has proven to be very reliable even though careful research techniques were not followed.

15. Dow, *History of Topsfield*, p. 37

16. There are several sources that indicate this possibility including newspaper articles in the Boston Globe in 1939 and in the Tri-Town Transcript in 1938 as well as entries in www.ancestry.com and at the Topsfield Historical Society. Also, an e-mail received by the author from John Quigley, February, 2002.

17. Dwinell, Ira, *Dwinell Genealogy*

18. Dwinell, Ira, *Dwinell Genealogy*

19. Correspondence from Merrill Dwinell to Governor Lane Dwinell with enclosures, 1958

20. Hayes, *Carlton J. H. History of Modern Europe to 1870*, pp. 251–276

21. Dwinell, Frank, Preface to the "Revised and Reprinted Genealogy of Ira Dwinell"

22. Research in the Tidewater area of Virginia in an effort to ascertain the arrival of Henry Dunnell on the Bonaventure in 1635

23. Lecture at the New England Genealogical Historical Society, Spring, 2003

24. Pioneer Irish in New England, p. 58, from www.ancestry.com. Also, there is a book written by Prendergast entitled *The Cromwellian Settlement*. The contention of this author is that thirteen and fourteen year old children were kidnapped off the streets of Ireland in the 1653–54 era and placed on a ship called the Goodfellow to be placed into indentured servitude in America. The Suffolk Deeds on file at the Massachusetts Archives show a man named George Dell was the Master of the Goodfellow. He was also part owner of the ship. There is a tie here. More research is needed in the Suffolk Deeds or

elsewhere to find a better connection between George Dell and Lieutenant Appleton of Ipswich. This tie would better support the Irish contention.

25. Prendergast, John P. *The Cromwellian Settlement in Ireland*, Constable, London, 1922

26. "Pioneer Irish in New England", found at <u>www.ancestry.com</u>

27. *Records and Files of the Quarterly Courts of Essex, Massachusetts, Vol. II,* 1656– 1662, Salem, Massachusetts Essex Institute, 1912, p. 41

28. Pioneer Irish of New England, p. 58, Many sources point to the diary that Solomon Dwinell wrote regarding his service in the Revolutionary War. I have seen this diary in a Worcester, Massachusetts, Library and did not find an Irish reference. Solomon's grandson, Solomon Ashley Dwinell, has claimed to be of Irish descent. He was a Congregational minister in Wisconsin who helped settle that area. He was a strong abolitionist. In a dedication to his career in Wisconsin a chronicler of the era indicated that he has heard Solomon Ashley Dwinell make a claim as to his Irish descent.

29. www.ancestry.com

30. Transplantation Certificate, dated 1653

31. Libre 1, pages 196–200, Suffolk Deeds

32. There are several reference in both London and Dublin giving permission to Sellick and Leader for this activity.

33. Pioneer Irish of New England mentions the connection between Mikal and Samuel Appleton in several places.

34. There is a classic case Involving Samuel Symonds of Topsfield who produced a Bill of Sale from George Dell regarding two of his servants—William Dalton and Edward Welch. The Bill of Sale provided for an 11-year indenture. The custom was a five to seven year indenture. The Bill of Sale prevailed.

35. This matter is also described on page 55 of Pioneer Irish in New England

36. Records and Files of the Ipswich Quarterly Court, 1668, page 5.

37. My personal DNA results from the Genographic Study of the National Geographic Society tracing my DNA back through history. This Project was brought to my attention through an article in the March, 2004, National Geographic Magazine. The Genographic Project Leader, Spencer Wells, has written an excellent, easy to read book entitled *The Journey of Man.* He explains the use of DNA as he traces the Y chromosome of male descendents back to our origin in Africa. His Project has traced my personal DNA back to a Celtic source. There is an excellent bibliography in Spencer's book that provides more technical information for the reader who would want to delve deeply into this subject.

38. MacManus, Seumas, *The Story of the Irish Race,* The Devin-Adair Company, Old Greenwich, Connecticut, 1921, Chapters one and two.

39. Morgan, Edmund S., "Masters & Servants From The Puritan Family" Part 1 of 2, 1944, Transcribed by Janice Farnsworth, www.rootsweb.com

40. www.rootsweb.com, Farnsworth

41. Dow, *History of Topsfield*

42. Consensus of five members of the Topsfield Historical Society, July, 2003

43. My wife and I had the opportunity to meet two women on a recent cruise. They were mother and daughter who were American citizens of Dutch origin. Jackie, the daughter of Tina, asked me how her daughter would be identified. I told her that she and her mother would be American citizens born in Holland. Her daughter would be an American born American citizen. I also told her that I was a ninth generation American of undetermined European origin.

44. Junger, Sebastian, *The Perfect Storm*, Harper Paperbacks, New York, 1998, pp. 97–101, 115;, 153–158

45. Morgan, Ted, *Wilderness at Dawn*, Touchstone, New York, 1993, p. 111

46. Morgan, Ted, *Wilderness at Dawn*, p. 138

47. "Passengers to Virginia", p. 82

48. Dutton, Benjamin, *Navigation and Nautical Astronomy*, 10th Edition, United States Naval Institute, 1951, p. 45

49. Bruce, Nona B., Bullock, James, "The Fort at No. 4–1740–1760, Fort at No. 4 Living History Museum, Charlestown, N.H., 1990, p. 1

50. Roll, Eric, *Modern Economic Thought*, Prentice Hall, New York, 1946, Chapter III

51. Dunnell, Henry Gale, *True Genealogy of the Dunnell and Dwinell Family*

52. Dow, George, *History of Topsfield*, p. 21

53. Dow, George, *History of Topsfield*, 8

54. Pettingill, Samuel, *The Yankee Pioneers a Saga of Courage*, Charles Tuttle Publishers, Rutland, Vermont, p. 21

55. Foster, David, "New England Forests Through Time", Lecture at the Squam Lake Science Center, Holderness, N.H., Summer, 2002

56. Pettingill, Samuel, *Yankee Pioneers a Saga of Courage*, p. 39

57. Allen, Mel, "Secrets of Trophy Trees", *Yankee Magazine*, Sept., 1999, p. 56

58. Foster, David, "New England Forests Through Time", Lecture

59. Everett, Robert T. "Update on Old-Growth Forests in Southern New England", www.massco.org. Conservation Perspectives, the on-line journal of MASSCB, winter, 2001, p. 8

60. Pettingill, Samuel, *Yankee Pioneers a Saga of Courage*, p. 39

61. Johnson, Edward, *Wonder Working Providence of Sion's Saviour in New England*

62. Hayes, Carlton J.H., *Modern Europe to 1870*, footnote on p. 69

63. Churchill, Winston, *The Birth of Britain*, Dodd Mead and Company, New York, 1956, pp 88–103

64. Dow, George, *History of Topsfield*, p. 98

65. Pettingill, Samuel, *Yankee Pioneers a Saga of Courage*, p. 83

66. Dow, George, *History of Topsfield*, p. 3

67. Pettingill, Samuel, *Yankee Pioneers a Saga of Courage*, p. 83

68. Foster, David, "New England Forests Through Time", Lecture

69. "Weather Events—The Great Hurricane of 1635 and the Legend of Thacker Island", www.islandnet.com, pp. 1–5

70. Foster, David, "Conservation Lessons and Challenges from Ecological History", Reprinted from *Forest History of Today*, Fall, 2000

71. Pettingill, Samuel, *Yankee Pioneers a Saga of Courage*, p. 83

72. Pettingill, Samuel, *Yankee Pioneers a Saga of Courage*, pp. 82 and 83

73. Foster, David, "New England Forests Through Time", Lecture

74. Personal observation of the author suggested by Dr. Foster.

75. "A Few Easily Accessible Areas of Old Growth Forest Open to the Public", www.wfer.org

76. Pettingill, Samuel, *Yankee Pioneers a Saga of Courage*, p. 38, p. 47

77. DeSorgher, Richard, Leighton, Barbara and Meany, Marjorie, "The Peak House Its Inhabitants and the Settlement of Medfield", Medfield Historical Society, Medfield, Massachusetts

78. Morgan, Ted, *Wilderness at Dawn*, pp. 131–151

79. Dow, George, *History of Topsfield*, pp. 84 and 85

80. Dow, George, *History of Topsfield*, p. 85

81. Dow, George, *History of Topsfield*, p. 9

82. Pettingill, Samuel, *Yankee Pioneers a Saga of Courage*, pp. 82 and 83

83. Morgan, Ted, *Wilderness at Dawn*, pp. 133–151

84. "Were They Shorter Then?", Average Heights, Plimouth on web, <u>www. plimouth.org</u>

85. Pettingill, Samuel, *Yankee Pioneers a Saga of Courage*, p. 92

86. Dow, George, *History of Topsfield*, See Index

87. Dow, George, *History of Topsfield*, p. 78

88. Pettingill, Samuel, *Yankee Pioneers a Saga of Courage*, pp. 42–50

89. Essex Probate Record, Submitter: John Quigley, <u>www.ancestry.com</u>

Chapter 2:

1. Dunnell, Henry Gale, *The True Dunnell, Dwinell Genealogy*, Charles B. Richardson, New York, 1862, pp. 8–10

2. Dwinell, Ira, *Dwinell Genealogy*

3. Dow, George Francis, *History of Topsfield*, p. 85

4. Ipswich Deeds, pages 185–187, 1672

5. Dunnell, Henry Gale, *The True Dunnell, Dwinell Genealogy*, pp. 6 and 7

6. Dow, George Francis, *History of Topsfield*

7. Dwinell, Ira, *Dwinell Genealogy*

8. Giampoli, Joan, *Descendants of Michael Dwinell*, Revised November 26, 2000, self published

9. Dow, George Francis, *History of Topsfield*, p. 420

10. Norton, Mary Beth, *In The Devil's Snare*, Alfred Knopf, New York, 2003

11. Dow, George Francis, *History of Topsfield*, p. 78

12. Dow, George Francis, *History of Topsfield*, p. 92 and 93

13. Puritanism, Puritans, <u>http://mb~soft.com/believe/</u>, p.3

14. Boyer, Paul and Nissenbaum, Stephen, *Salem Possessed*, Harvard University Press, Cambridge, Massachusetts, 1974

15. Hill, Frances, *A Delusion of Satan*, Doubleday, New York, 1943, p. 36

16. Hill, Frances, *A Delusion of Satan*, p. 36

17. Norton, Mary Beth, In The Devil's Snare, p. 21

18. Boyer, Paul and Nissenbaum, Stephen, *The Salem Witch Craft Papers*, Vol. 2 verbatim transcripts of the legal documents of the Salem witchcraft outbreak of 1692/edited with an introduction and index by Paul Boyer and Stephen Nissenbaum, Electronic Text Center, University of Virginia Library, http://etext.hb/virginia.ed.

19. Dow, George Francis, *History of Topsfield*, Chapter XIX

20. Norton, Mary Beth, *In the Devil's Snare*, pp. 295–298 (She points out religious influences but contends the existence of a war-like environment dominated secular thought.)

21. Towne, Abbie Peterson (Mrs.), and Clark, Marietta, (Miss), "Topsfield in the Witchcraft Delusion", Vol. XIII, Topsfield Historical Society, Topsfield, Massachusetts, 1908, pp. 3

22. Dow, George Francis, *A History of Topsfield*, pp. 324–340

23. Dow, George Francis, *A History of Topsfield*, p. 339–340

24. Dow, George Francis, *A History of Topsfield*

25. Dow, George Francis, *History of Topsfield*,

26. Dow, George Francis, *Town Records of Topsfield, Massachusetts.*, Topsfield Historical Society, Topsfield, Massachusetts

27. Dow, George Francis, *History of Topsfield*

28. *Hippocrates Writings*, Franklin Center, Penn.

29. Long, Henry Follansbee, "The Physicians of Topsfield With Some Accounts of Early Medical Practice"

30. Long Henry Follansbee, "The Physicians of Topsfield With Some Accounts of Early Medical Practice"

31. Roll, Eric, A History of Economic Thought, York, p. 58

32. Churchill, Winston, The Birth of Britain, Dodd and Mead and Company, N.Y., pp. 162–165

33. Churchill, Winston, *The Birth of Britain*, pp. 162–165

34. Churchill, Winston, *The Birth of Britain*, .

35. Churchill, Winston, *The Birth of Britain*,

36. Churchill, Winston, *The Birth of Britain*, pp. 173–176

37. Churchill, Winston, *The Birth of Britain*, Chapter Thirteen, "The English Common Law"

38. Roll, Eric, *A History of Economic Thought*

Chapter three:

1. Dwinell, Ira, *The Dwinell Genealogy*

2. Dwinell, Ira, *The Dwinell Genealogy*

3. Dow, George Francis, *History of Topsfield*, p. 339

4. Dwinell, Ira, *The Dwinell Genealogy*

5. Dwinell, Ira, *The Dwinell Genealogy*

6. Dwinell, Ira, *The Dwinell Genealogy*

7. Dow, George Francis, *History of Topsfield*, pp. 135 and 136

8. Dow, George Francis, *History of Topsfield*, p. 150

9. Anderson, Fred, *A Peoples Army: Massachusetts Soldiers and Society in the Seven Years' War, p. 8*

10. Ketchum, Richard, *The Battle for Bunker Hill*, Doubleday & Company, Inc., New York, 1962, p. 87

11. Dow, George Francis, *History of Topsfield*, p. 154

12. Anderson, Fred, A People's Army: *Massachusetts Soldiers and Society in the Seven Years' War*, p. 66

13. Dow, George Francis, *History of Topsfield*, p. 156

14. *Massachusetts Archives*, Vol. 94, p. 386

15. *Massachusetts Archives*, Vol. 95

16. Cooper, James Fenimore, *The Last of the Mohicans*

17. Steele, Ian, *Betrayals*, p. 85

18. Bruce, Nona B. and Bullock, Barbara Jones, *The Fort at No. 4 1740–1760*, Fort at No. 4 Living History Museum, Charlestown, N.H., 1990, p. 8

19. Anderson, Fred, *A Peoples' Army: Massachusetts Soldiers and Society in the Seven Years' War*, pp. 94–97

20. Anderson, Fred, *A Peoples' Army: Massachusetts Soldiers and Society in the Seven Years' War*, pp. 38 and 39

21. Dow, George Francis, *A History of Topsfield*, p. 158

22. Anderson, Fred, *A Peoples' Army: Massachusetts Soldiers and Society in the Seven Years' War*, p. 123

23. Anderson, Fred, *A Peoples' Army: Massachusetts Soldiers and Society in the Seven Years' War*, pp. 27and 28

24. Anderson, Fred, *A Peoples' Army: Massachusetts Soldiers and Society in the Seven Years' War*, pp. 27 and 28

25. Anderson, Fred, *A Peoples' Army: Massachusetts Soldiers and Society in the Seven Years' War*, p. 141

26. Anderson, Fred, *A Peoples' Army: Massachusetts Soldiers and Society in the Seven Years' War*, p. 36

27. Ferguson, E. James, "Currency Finance: An Interpretation of Colonial Monetary Practices", *American Economic History, Essays in Interpretation*, edited by Coben, Stanley and Hill, Forest G., J.B. Lippincott Company, Philadelphia, 1966, p. 96

28. Anderson, Fred, *A Peoples' Army: Massachusetts Soldiers and Society in the Seven Years' War, p. 32–39*

29. *Massachusetts Archives*, Vol. 95, p.

30. Morison, Samuel Eliot, *The Oxford History of the American People*, PP. 345–347

31. Anderson, Fred, *A Peoples' Army: Massachusetts Soldiers and Society in the Seven Years' War*, pp. 187–189

32. Anderson, Fred, A Peoples' *Army: Massachusetts Soldiers and Society in the Seven Years' War, p. 223*

33. Raphael, Ray, *The First American Revolution Before Lexington and Concord*, The New Press, New York, 2002, p. 10

34. Raphael, Ray, *The First American Revolution Before Lexington and Concord*, pp. 23–27

35. Raphael, Ray, *The First American Revolution Before Lexington and Concord*, pp. 23–27

36. Levy, Leonard W., *Origins of the Bill of Rights*, Yale University Press, New Haven, Connecticut, 1999, Chapters 1 and 2

37. Perley, Sidney, *History of Boxford, Massachusetts*, Boxford, Massachusetts, 1880

38. Zinn, Howard, *A People's History of the United States*, Harper Collins Publishers, New York, 2003, p. 77

39. Galvin, John, *The Minutemen, the First Fight, Myths and Realities of the American Revolution*, 2nd Edition, Revised, Pergamon, N.Y., 1989, p. 2

40. Perley, Sidney, *History of Boxford, Massachusetts*

41. Rafeal, Ray, *The First American Revolution Before Lexington and Concord*, p. 21

Chapter four:

1. Dwinell, Ira, *The Dwinell Genealogy*

2. Perley, Sidney, *History of Boxford, Massachusetts*

3. *Map of Boxford*, Provided by the Boxford Historical Society

4. Anderson, Fred, *A People's Army: Massachusetts Soldiers and Society in the Seven Years' War, pp. 222 and 223*

5. Churchill, Winston, *Birth of Britain*, pp. 215–225, 242–257, Also, *The Age of Revolution*, pp. 166 and 167

6. Morison, Samuel Eliot, *The Oxford History of the American People*, pp. 172

7. Handlin, Oscar, *The History of the United States*, Volume One, Holt, Rinehart and Winston, New York, 1983, p. 194

8. Handlin, Oscar, *The History of the United States*, Volume One, p. 194

9. Morison, Samuel Eliot, *The Oxford History of the American People*, p. 182 and 183

10. Morison, Samuel Eliot, *The Oxford History of the American People*, p. 190

11. Morison, Samuel Eliot, *The Oxford History of the American People*, p. 184

12. Morison, Samuel Eliot, *The Oxford History of the American People*, p. 180

13. Raphael, Ray, *The First American Revolution Before Lexington and Concord, pp.10 and 11*

14. Morison, Samuel Eliot, *The Oxford History of the American People*, p. 177

15. McCullough, David, *John Adams,* Simon and Shuster, New York, 2001, p. 60

16. Raphael, Ray, *The First American Revolution Before Lexington and Concord*, pp. 43–45

17. Raphael, Ray, *The First American Revolution Before Lexington and Concord*, pp. 41 and 42

18. Raphael, Ray, *The First American Revolution Before Lexington and Concord*, pp. 33–35

19. Raphael, Ray, *The First American Revolution Before Lexington and Concord*, p. 10

20. Raphael, Ray, *The First American Revolution Before Lexington and Concord*, pp. 90 and 91

21. Raphael, Ray, *The First American Revolution Before Lexington and Concord*, pp. 181–183

22. Gross, Robert A., *The Minutemen and Their World,* Hill and Wang, N.Y., 1976, p. 59

23. Gross, Robert A., *The Minutemen and Their World*, p. 68 and 69

24. Gross, Robert A., *The Minutemen and Their World*, p. 68

25. Galvin, John R., *The Minutemen, First Fight, Myths and Realities of the American Revolution,* 2nd Edition, Revised, Pergamon, N.Y., 1989 pp. 132, 234, 241 and 242

26. N.H. Revolutionary War Pension Records, Supplement Series, Volume 6-D, pp. 159–161

27. Ketchum, Richard M., *The Battle for Bunker Hill,* p. 72

28. Ketchum, Richard M., *The Battle for Bunker Hill,* p. 71

29. Ketchum, Richard M., *The Battle for Bunker Hill,* p. 71

30. Ketchum, Richard M., *The Battle for Bunker Hill,* pp. 68 and 69

31. Ketchum, Richard M., *The Battle for Bunker Hill*, pp. 73–79

32. Ketchum, Richard M., *The Battle for Bunker Hill*, p. 81

33. Symonds, Craig L. and Clipson, William J., *A Battlefield Atlas of the Revolution*, The Nautical and Aviation Publishing Company of America, Inc., 1986, Annapolis, Maryland, pp. 18 and 19

34. Ketchum, Richard M., *The Battle for Bunker Hill*, pp. 90 and 91

35. Symonds, Craig L. and Clipson, William J., *A Battlefield Atlas of the Revolution*, pp. 18 and 19

36. Ketchum, Richard M., *The Battle for Bunker Hill*

37. Symonds, Craig L. and Clipson, William J. *A Battlefield Atlas of the Revolution*, pp. 18 and 19

38. *N.H. Revolutionary Pension Records*, Supplement Series, Vol. 6-D, pp. 159–161

39. *N.H. Revolutionary Pension Records*, Supplement Series, Vol. 6-D, pp. 159–161

40. Dwinell, Ira, *The Dwinell Genealogy*

41. Griffin, S. G., *A History of Keene*, Sentinel Printing Company, Keene, N.H., 1904, p. 204

42. Griffin, S. G., *A History of Keene*, p. 219

43. Griffin, S. G., *A History of Keene*, p. 219

44. Griffin, S. G., *A History of Keene*, p. 219

45. Stabler, Lois K., Editor, *Very Poor and of a Lo Make*, The Journal of Albert Sanger, Historical Society of Cheshire County and Peter E. Randall, Publisher, Portsmouth, N.H., 1986, p. 370

46. Griffin, S. G., *A History of Keene*, p.458

47. Stabler, Lois K, *Very Poor and of a Lo Make*, p. 414 (footnote)

48. Stabler, Lois K., *Very Poor and of a Lo Make*, p. 437

49. Stabler, Lois K., *Very Poor and of a Lo Make*, p. 367

50. Griffin, S. G., *A History of Keene*, p. 300

51. Stebbins, Sarah Dwinell, *Genealogical Notes.* 1919

52. Dwinell, Ira, *Dwinell Genealogy*

53. Stabler, Lois K., *Very Poor and of a Lo Make*, p. 437

54. Hill, Ralph Nading, *Yankee Kingdom Vermont and New Hampshire,* Harper and Row, N.Y., 1960, p. 126

Chapter 5

1. GloverDeeds, Book 2, page 259 (In Vermont Land Deeds are located in the Clerk's office of each Town. The deeds mentioned are Glover, Vermont, deeds

2. Vigilante, Sylvester, "Eighteen-Hundred-and-Froze-to-Death", *Mischief in the Mountains,* edited by Hard, Walter R., Jr. and Greene, Janet C., Vermont Life Magazine, Montpelier, Vermont, 1970 (This is an oft-repeated story found in many other sources.)

3. History of the Town of Glover, Vermont, Glover Bicentennial Committee, Burlington, Vermont, p. 135

4. History of Glover, p. 3

5. History of Glover, p. 126

6. Pettingill, Samuel, *Yankee Pioneer A Saga in Courage*, Charles E. Tuttle Company, Rutland, Vermont, p. 54

7. *Yankee Pioneer A Saga of Courage*, Charles E. Tuttle and Co., 1971, p. Pettingill, Samuel, *Yankee Pioneers a Saga in Courage*, p. 73

8. Stebbins, Sarah Dwinell, Genealogical Notes, 1909

9. Dwinell, Ira, *The Dwinell Genealogy*

10. Dwinell, Ira, *The Dwinell Genealogy*

11. Pettingill, Samuel, *Yankee Pioneers a Saga in Courage*, p. 45

12. History of Glover, pp. 1 and 2

13. Pettingill, Samuel, *Yankee Pioneers a Saga in Courage*, p. 100

14. Samuelson, Paul, *Economics*, 4th Edition, McGraw Hill Book Company, N.Y., 1958, pp. 26 and 27

15. History of Glover, p. 11

16. Some of Solomon's transactions: Book 2, p. 260; Book 2, p. 339; Book 4, p. 77

17. Book 6, page 485

18. Book 7, page 327, Also, Book 10, p. 212

19. Book 12, page 60

20. Dwinell, Ira, *The Dwinell Genealogy*

21. Dwinell, Ira, *The Dwinell Genealogy*

22. History of Glover, p. 8

23. Dwinell, Ira, *The Dwinell Genealogy*

24. Dow, David, A Clockmaker who is an authority on Antique Clocks, Grafton, Massachusetts, circa 1995

25. Dwinell, Ira, *The Dwinell Genealogy*

26. Dwinell, Ira, *The Dwinell Genealogy*

27. Dwinell, Ira, *The Dwinell Genealogy*

28. Book 7 page 327 and Book 10, p. 212

29. Hill, Ralph Nading, *Yankee Kingdom Vermont and New Hampshire*, p. 161

30. History of Glover, p. 132

31. Dwinell, Ira, *The Dwinell Genealogy*

32. Hill, Ralph Nading, *Yankee Kingdom Vermont and New Hampshire*, P.211

33. Dwinell, Alice, Conversation, 2003

34. Hemenway, Abba Maria, *Vermont Historical Magazine*, p. 201

35. Book 12, page 60

36. History of Glover, p. 128

37. Obituary notice for Julia Dwinell, The Caledonian, in 1893

38. Dwinell, Ira, *The Dwinell Genealogy*

39. Dwinell, Ira, *The Dwinell Genealogy*

40. Dwinell, Ira, *The Dwinell Genealogy*

41. History of Glover, Several references

42. Obituary Notice for Julia Dwinell

43. Dwinell, Ira, *The Dwinell Genealogy*

44. Dwinell, Ira, *The Dwinell Genealogy*

45. There are several references for this quote

46. Dwinell, Ira, *The Dwinell Genealogy*

47. Class of 1896, St. Johnsbury Academy 50th Reunion, p. 27

48. Dwinell, Ira, *The Dwinell Genealogy*

49. History of Glover, pp. 38 and 46

50. Book 17 page 185 and 186

51. Dwinell, Ira, *The Dwinell Genealogy*

52. Dwinell, Ira, *The Dwinell Genealogy*

53. Papers related to the Probate of the estates of Joseph Dwinell and Ann Dwinell. These papers are in the Probate Court of Newport or among the deeds of the Glover, Vermont, town clerk's office, depending upon the nature of the document.

54. An analysis of several deeds from 1891 to 1910

55. Dwinell, Ira, *The Dwinell Genealogy*

56. Registration Card and Registrar's Report, Lowell, Massachusetts, 1917. This was the obligatory registration for the World War I draft.

57. Dwinell, Ira, *The Dwinell Genealogy*

58. Schlesinger, Arthur M., Jr., *Crisis of the Old Order*, pp. 210–223

Chapter Six:

1. Dwinell, Ira, The Dwinell Genealogy

2. Lane Dwinell gave this photograph to Roy Black. It came from a Newport, Vermont, newspaper.

3. Bartlett, K.S., Boston Sunday Globe article, November 14, 1954.

4. Hart, Jeffrey, The Dartmouth Review, April 16, 1997

5. Zinn, Howard, *A People's History of the United States*, Perennial Classics, New York, 2003, p. 430

6. Shlesinger, Arthur M., Jr., *Crisis of the Old Order*, Houghton Mifflin Company, Boston, p. 223

7. www.unhmagazine.unh.edu, "Courage Under Fire"

8. This journal came after his experience at the University of New Hampshire. The name of the journal is the Monthly Review.

9. "A Distinguished Rail Fan", Railroad Magazine, August, 1955, p. 64

10. Dwinell, Ira, *The Dwinell Genealogy*

11. "Eleanor D. Borella Dies Tuesday At 64", The Valley News, Lebanon, NH, Nov. 1975

12. "Miss Dwinell Is Bride to New York Man", The Granite State News, Volume 89, April, 19, 1934

13. http//groups.msn.com, "Armies: Patton's Slapping Incident", p. 9

14. "Eleanor D. Borella Dies Tuesday at 64"

15. Dwinell, Ira, *The Dwinell Genealogy*

16. Dwinell, Carl M. "Class of 1896", St. Johnsbury Academy 1896–1946, p. 27

17. Newport Daily News, Jan. 4, 1976 Also, http://ep.espacenet.com (The latter is a web site for the specific information regarding a patent award.)

18. Dwinell, Ira, *The Dwinell Genealogy*

19. Dwinell, Ira, *The Dwinell Genealogy*

20. An excellent description of this subject is provided in Dorothy Canfield Fisher's *Vermont Traditions,* Boston, 1953

21. Dwinell, Ira, The Dwinell Genealogy

22. www.ww11memorial.com, Also, www.arlingtoncemetery.net/eehume

23. www.milforddailynews.com, Kim, Eunice, Oct. 26, 2004

24. Sidebar table in the Boston Globe showing the lowest temperatures for Boston in available U.S. Weather Bureau Records, February, 2000

25. www.mhp.net

26. www.freepatentsonline.com

978-0-595-45091-6
0-595-45091-1